Abductions

Allison Lewis

Published by Trellis Publishing, 2021.

While every precaution has been taken in the preparation of this book, the publisher assumes no responsibility for errors or omissions, or for damages resulting from the use of the information contained herein.

ABDUCTIONS

First edition. July 11, 2021.

ISBN: 979-8224080878

Written by Allison Lewis.

ABDUCTIONS

Allison Lewis

HOLLY BOBO

Holly Bobo had the brightest of futures. She had everything a young woman could ask for; a great circle of friends, a devoted boyfriend and a loving family. Growing up in the tiny town of Darden, Tennessee, she was involved in church where she sang like an angel every Sunday. She was the first cousin of country singer Whitney Duncan so the talent for entertainment was in the genes. But the blonde girl with the angelic smile wanted to serve people first hand so she enrolled in the nursing program at the University of Tennessee. Up until April 13th, 2011, the 20 year old's life could not be better

On April 13th, 2011, everything changed.

Holly had set her alarm for 4:30 a.m. that morning as she had to do some last minute cramming for one of her nursing classes. The morning started off like any other, she got up, ate breakfast, studied and dressed. At 7:30 a.m. she took a short phone call from Drew Scott, her boyfriend. Drew was nearby doing some early morning turkey hunting on Holly's grandmother's property. The two exchanged pleasantries with the loving boyfriend wishing her well on the upcoming exam. Both of Holly's parents left for work and her brother Clint had not awakened just yet.

Ten minutes later, Holly's neighbor heard the sound of the young woman screaming. The neighbor called Karen Bobo (Holly's mother) at her job and stated that she heard some screaming at her residence. The screaming caused the family dogs to start barking which awakened Clint. Peering out of a crack in his blinds he saw a man with Holly outside. He saw Holly kneeling down next to Drew. "They looked like they were kneeled down," Clint said. "Facing each other in the garage, and they were talking back and forth. Holly sounded very upset and heated. He was doing much of the talking, and she would answer back and things like that. I couldn't make out hardly any of the words. The only words I could make out from here were Holly saying, 'No, why?'"

Clint and Drew were best friends and he wrote off the incident as a typical argument between couples. Deciding that it was not any of his business, he left them to it and didn't give the scene he had just witnessed much thought for the time being. He was unaware that Drew was hunting at his grandmother's property and therefore could not have been the man arguing with Holly. The telephone rang and Clint answered – it was his panicked mother asking about Holly. Clint tried to explain what he had just seen taking place outside but Karen dismissed his claim.

"Clint!" Karen screamed. "That's not Drew. Get a gun and shoot him.'

Clint remained in denial. Still groggy from sleep and believing he saw Drew through the blinds, he argued back.

"You want me to shoot Drew? And I don't want to call 911 and say 'my sister and her boyfriend are breaking up.'"

Karen realized that she was getting nowhere fast with her son. She hung up on him and called 911 instead but precious minutes had past. To add to the confusion, her call was routed to the incorrect dispatcher due to the fact that she had called from work and her home was in another county.

Meanwhile back at the Bobo residence, Clint took another look outside. Now he saw Holly walking off into the woods with the man, whom he now realized was wearing camouflage. "The only thing I could see was his right arm, which was hanging down," Clint recalled as he watched his sister disappear into the woods. Heart pounding, he tried Holly's cell phone but it reached the voice ail. He then tried Drew on his cell to no avail.

At 8.00 a.m. Karen called Clint back. When he told her about the latest development Karen told Clint to call 911 and report it. Arming himself with a loaded pistol, Clint headed outside. He discovered a pool of blood next to his sister's car.

Clint finally called 911.

Police arrived as did Karen and a number of neighbors. Confusion abounded as everyone walked all of the crime scene and possibly compromising evidence.

"It seems like it was well over two hours at least before anyone went into the woods," Terri Brumley, a family friend said. "They waited on search dogs to get here and a helicopter."

"I was begging them to put out road blocks," Karen said. "The bond that Holly and I had - I knew that something was completely, absolutely wrong, but I just couldn't make anybody understand that."

The hunt for Holly Bobo thus began but it bore little fruit. Her lunch box was discovered about eight miles from the home while a shoeprint from a Croc's brand of foam clogs was discovered outside the house.

MEDIA FRENZY

The high level of media interest in the case had also led to a plethora of inaccurate tip-offs from well-meaning members of the public, as well as hundreds of leads from dozens of self-professed psychics, that investigators have had to wade through.

One psychic stated 'Bobo's abductor might have a scar on his forehead, or a rash on his elbow, or a bite mark on his hand. He might work from home as a graphic designer and long for the 1950s. His hair might be dark brown, or blonde, or salt and pepper. He might be clean shaven, or he might have a moustache. He might be a Scorpio. He is either scrawny, or of medium build, or stocky and muscular - possibly ex-military. He might own a black leather wallet and his name might contain one or more of the following letters: B, A, J, R, W or M. His last name might be Glenn. Bobo might be, or might have been at one point, in or near a place that has the number seven associated with it. Either an address or a highway number or possibly seven miles from some landmark.' Another psychic believed that the key to finding Holly was hidden within the lyrics of the Neil Diamond song 'September Morn.' Yet another psychic, stated with confidence on

April 14, 2011 that Holly would be found alive, that her captor makes a lot of mistakes and would be found within five days. Prominent television psychic profiler Carla Baron of 'Haunting Evidence' offered her services to the Bobo family pro bono, but they declined on the advice of the TBI.

THE ACCUSED

It would take nearly three years, March of 2014 to be exact, for any arrests to be made. Local brothers Zach and Dylan Adams, along with friend Jason Autry were taken into custody. The trio were charged with aggravated kidnapping, rape and murder in the first degree. Previously another two brothers, Mark and Jeffrey Pearcy, stood accused of tampering with evidence and accessory after the fact, but the charges against them were later dropped. A sixth man, Shayne Austin, was identified by investigators as a potential person of interest in the case, although formal charges were never filed. Austin committed suicide nearly a year after the trio were arrested.

THE BODY

On September 2014, Holly's remains would be found. Two hunters discovered her decomposed body near a logging road adjacent to County Corner Road in northern Decatur County, twenty miles from her home. Investigators broke the news at a 10.00 p.m. press conference held at the Decatur County Sheriff's Department. The remains were sent to the Tennessee Bureau of Investigation forensics laboratory in Memphis, which later determined that the remains were indeed that of Holly Bobo. The owner of the property where Holly's partial remains were located said that it was a regular occurrence for people to travel through his property without permission as it was a popular hunting ground. One of the hunters spotted a big bucket near the remains, which he emptied. He instantly regretted his decision. Information regarding whatever the man saw in the bucket has not been released to the general public. His only statement was that he remains haunted by what he saw.

Prosecutors would seek the death penalty for Autry and the Adams brothers due to the fact that "the murder was especially heinous, atrocious or cruel in that it involved torture or serious physical abuse beyond that necessary to produce death;' was committed in aid of 'avoiding, interfering with, or preventing a lawful arrest or prosecution;' and was 'knowingly committed, solicited, directed or aided' by the accused."

Zach Adams was the first to be arrested and charged with Holly's murder. This was based on information provided to investigators by his brother Dylan, who told them that he had seen Holly, still alive, at the house he shared with his brother later on the same day that she was taken. He stated that he had gone home to retrieve his truck, and was surprised to find Holly Bobo seated in the living room wearing a pink t-shirt (Holly had indeed been wearing a pink t-shirt when she was last seen) with Jason Autry standing near her. He told investigators Zach was 'wearing camouflage shorts, black cut-off-sleeve t-shirt and a pair of green Crocs.' He further stated that Zach had informed him that 'he had raped Bobo and videotaped it.' No such tape was ever recovered in the search executed on the Adams residence by investigators. They did find a blond hair in a bedroom closet. It is not known if this hair came from Holly.

Jason Autry was the second man to be arrested and charged in connection to the Holly Bobo murder. He was charged with aggravated kidnapping and first-degree murder charges a month after Zach Adams. In May of 2015, a rape charge was also added. Autry faces the death penalty based purely on Dylan Adams' statement naming him as present with Holly Bobo at the Adams residence on the day of her abduction. No other evidence has surfaced to date.

Investigators offered Shayne Austin an immunity deal for any part he may have played in Holly's murder in exchange for information leading to the recovery of her remains. Police believed that Austin knew where Holly was buried and possibly assisted in the disposal of the body based on the fact that telephone records show that Zach Adams spoke to Austin several times on the date of Holly's abduction. The immunity agreement was taken off the table when Austin was unable to tell police what they wanted to know. In revoking the offer, the district attorney stated that Austin 'has not been completely truthful, forthcoming and cooperative as to any and all aspects of this investigation.' In April 2014, Austin's attorney filed an injunction request against prosecutors seeking to prevent them from laying charges. In February 2015, Austin committed suicide by hanging himself in a Bartow, Florida hotel room. His attorney pointed the blame squarely at investigators in the Bobo case due to what he termed their 'witch hunt' interrogation tactics, in that their investigation was based largely on hearsay and rumors from unreliable sources instead of actual evidence. The attorney maintains that his client had nothing to do with Holly's murder and that he cooperated with police to the best of his ability.

Investigators also set their sights on Dylan Adams, charging him with evidence tampering and disposal in September 2014. It is not known what specific evidence they were referring to but the charges were later dropped. He was later charged with rape based on a confession he allegedly made to police. Adams' attorney complained that the State has not yet turned over any evidence to him. In May 2015 Adams was further charged with especially aggravated rape, especially aggravated kidnapping and murder in the first degree. Again, any specific evidence against Adams, if any, has not been made known.

In July 2014 investigators charged brothers Jeff and Mark Pearcy with evidence tampering and accessory after the fact after Sandra King (Jeff's former roommate) alleged that two months prior Jeff had shown her a video in which Zach Adams assaulted a restrained and crying Holly Bobo, a video that Mark Pearcy supposedly filmed. Working with police, Sandra made a phone call to Jeff in an attempt to trap him into admitting to the existence of said video. While police listened in and recorded the phone call, Sandra said 'That video of Holly - if it had been you, I would have watched it,' to which Jeff replied 'I know.' The Pearcy brothers deny any involvement in the crime and the existence of such a video. Jeff maintained he does not even know Autry or the Adams brothers. Of his comment in the taped phone call, Jeff says that he was not able to hear Sandra clearly and that he thought that she was saying something about his ex-wife (also named Holly). Over twenty phones have been confiscated and searched but no such video has ever been found. All charges against the Pearcy brothers were later dropped. Supposedly District Attorney Matt Stowe, together with the Tennessee Bureau of Investigation, plan to charge more people with additional crimes in connection to the Holly Bobo murder, but he declined to elaborate on who these people or what these charges might be.

In spite of Dylan Adams' initial alleged statements, all three of the accused maintain their innocence in relation to the crimes. Jason Autry said in a media interview in May of 2014 'I want to let them know they have an innocent man right here. I'm a drug addict and a thief, but I'm not a killer.' Autry went on to allege that Dylan, who was already serving a jail sentence on unrelated gun charges, made up the story about him and Zach due to bad blood between the brothers and also in the hope of gaining a reduction on his sentence – 'They hate each other's guts and that's a way to get back at him.' Autry also alleges that investigators attempted to coerce him into providing false testimony about Zach Adams.

Dylan's family says that investigators are taking advantage of his low IQ and mental disabilities in order to coerce a fabricated confession that suits their agenda, with a family spokesperson telling reporters that Dylan 'has the mind of a child. They kept him up all night, would not give him anything to eat or drink and finally he said "What do you want me to say?" The family says Dylan can barely read, cannot perform basic tasks like telling the time, getting a false confession out of him would be no more difficult than getting a false confession out of a child.

Similarly, Jeff Pearcy alleges that Sandra King's statements were nothing more than a desperate attempt to leverage a reduction in prison time for her son, who at the time had served fourteen years of a thirty-eight year prison sentence – 'I have been up front and honest about everything. I have willingly given them everything. Take it, I mean, it's there. My heart goes out to the Bobo family. It could have very well been one of my kids. For someone to give them false hope, and that's exactly what's been done to them. But for the justice system to just haul someone in and destroy their whole life, I mean, there's no sense in that at all.'

John Herbison, Autry's attorney, has leveled criticism at the investigation into his client – 'I don't think the state has any case against Jason Autry. If those reports are correct, it means that they're just playing games. They charged him with something less serious in order to keep him locked up, and then when it comes time to answer questions about the charge, they dismiss that and charge him with a more serious charge in circuit court, where he's not entitled to a preliminary hearing.' In response to the prosecution's claim that they only dropped the charges against Mark Pearcy because he was facing unrelated federal charges which took precedence, Herbison said 'If the state is claiming that is the case, the prosecutor is either ill-informed or being disingenuous.'

The prosecution's handling of the case against the accused has been heavily criticized by leading legal experts. It has been marked by the seemingly arbitrary addition and removal of charges at random or as some sort of posturing or game playing on their part, as well as in-fighting between members of the prosecution which has further complicated the case. Indeed, to the outside observer it appears to have been a bumbling affair at several stages of the investigation and prosecution. One might even say that it has descended into the level of farce at times. District Attorney Matt Stowe rose to office in the summer of 2014. He publicly attributed a large part of the rationale for his election as being due to the thus-far bungled murder investigation - 'Voters wanted another set of eyes on this Holly Bobo case. They weren't happy with everything that was coming out of there, and I think that they wanted someone else to take a look and someone else to say "We know what's going on."

They say the wheels of justice turn slowly, but after the prosecution missed several evidence discovery deadlines and appeared to be deliberately and unnecessarily delaying the case, it proved to be too slowly for no-nonsense Judge Creed McGinley, who warned the prosecution 'I am absolutely out of patience with these cases not moving' in ordering that the case against Zach Adams be filed within one week and that evidence discovery take place immediately on December 17, 2014. The prosecution brazenly ignored the judge and his deadlines. Attorneys for the accused filed motions to dismiss, accusing the prosecution of 'silence or stonewalling' on a long list of complaints that also included failure to disclose forensic evidence that the skull found in the woods actually was that of Holly Bobo. Autry's attorney criticized 'It would appear to me if they had a skull with a dental match they would have given that to us right away. It's a little suspicious why we don't have that forensic information.'

In July of 2015, attorneys for the accused finally received access to the state's evidence against their clients. John Herbison filed a subpoena forcing Matt Stowe and TBI director Mark Gwyn to testify at a hearing in relation to the in-house disputes among the TBI and to provide an answer as to why the prosecution was intentionally stalling the case for such an unusually excessive amount of time. Following this December 2015 hearing regarding the bumbling TBI case, the TBI dropped the investigation and severed ties with the district in response to accusations of misconduct made by Matt Stowe. The TBI agreed to resume its investigation after Stowe recused himself and special prosecutor Jennifer Nichols was installed in his place. In response to this turn of events, attorneys for the accused now plan to subpoena Stowe in order to question him about the specifics of his misconduct allegations. Emails written by Wall Kirby, the Executive Director of the Tennessee District Attorney's Conference, exposed some of Stowe's concerns, specifically that the case was moving 'so slowly that the culprits were always one step ahead and that the TBI was leaking information and possibly covering up evidence.'

A hearing set for August 26, 2015 was cancelled so that attorneys for the accused would have a chance to examine evidence belatedly provided by the prosecution. John Herbison speculated that a new date for the hearing might be some time away. The date was eventually set for April 3, 2017, nearly six years after Holly's abduction.

The case has been the subject of intense national media interest, at some times to the detriment of the investigation when inaccuracies have been reported. Holly was first said to have been dragged into the woods by Camo Man. Clint Bobo later stated that this was not the case and that Holly walked into the woods with the man, either willingly or by force. This and other seemingly questionable statements and decisions made by Clint have led to a trial in the court of public opinion, with a popular theory being that Clint killed Holly, or was involved in the murder plot, and has changed his story at times. Questions such as: Why did he just stand by and watch his sister get abducted? Why didn't he listen to his mother? Why did he not pursue the abductor? There has also been a lot of speculation from the public as to Clint's mental capacity. Whitney Duncan took to Twitter on April 17, 2011 to defend Clint, stating 'My cousin Clint, Holly's brother, is NOT a suspect & I'm sick of people saying that he is. He has been cleared for good reason. Shut up.' In turn, police then later clarified that this was not the case. While the investigation was not focusing on Clint, nobody had been 'cleared' as a suspect at that stage.

In actuality, as the sole witness to Holly's abduction, naturally Clint faced some scrutiny. He has taken polygraph tests, been hypnotized, interrogated for more than seventeen hours, handed his cell phone and hard drive over to police and been strip searched (the TBI denied this ever took place). He has received death threats and accusations from people who believe that he killed his sister. Karen Bobo told the media 'They're (people who accuse Clint) warped. In my mind, they're warped.'

It has never been revealed what, if any, previous connection Holly had with her abductors. Her family remained stoic throughout the trials of the accused. They were satisfied with the life sentences imposed on them, not wanting to hear the gory details of what their daughter went through.

CHARLES LINDBERGH

14

JASMINE GREY

On March 1, 1932, Charles Lindbergh Jr. was taken from his bedroom, killed, and dumped in some nearby woods. All without anyone inside the house hearing a single peep. It was a case that gripped the entire nation, and baffled many for years.

Although one man was charged and executed for the crime, well into the 21st century many still doubt he acted alone. While many modern investigators continue to try to piece the events of that eventful night together to discover the truth, whether we will ever know truly what happened that evening remains to be seen.

The crime would touch a fear lurking in every parent: somehow, without warning or reason, their child would be taken from them. Never to return.

Never before had a child this celebrated and adored been so shockingly victimized.

Chapter one

Charles Lindbergh was a hero in his own time. At the age of 25, in 1927 Lindbergh did the impossible—he completed the first ever solo nonstop transatlantic flight. He instantly became a household name and a global icon. With his big blue eyes, Lindbergh personified the best of America. He was young, handsome, tall, and a bit shy. He was irresistible to the world in that moment.

The same year as his transatlantic flight, Lindbergh met Anne Morrow, the daughter of Lindbergh's financial adviser, while on a goodwill tour in Mexico. The two instantly hit it off and were married two years later at Anne's family estate in Englewood. The next year, the pair's life seemingly became complete when they had their first child, Charles Lindbergh Jr. It was a happy day, and the newlyweds were looking forward to a happy future together.

But their happily-ever-after never came.

Charles Lindbergh and Anne Morrow Lindbergh purchased a rural family home just outside of Hopewell, New Jersey. The couple and their infant son, Charles Lindbergh Jr. spent their weekend in the new house, but during the week they stayed at Anne's family estate in Englewood. The Hopewell property was under heavy construction and wasn't fit for the family to live there full time.

On the night of his kidnapping, Charles Lindbergh Jr. was put to bed in his second-story bedroom around 8:00pm by the family nurse Betty Gow. Gow took care to tuck the young boy in extra tight so he would be safe and sound throughout the night. Charles Jr. was sick, so the family stayed at the Hopewell property into the week—it was a Tuesday night—so they didn't have to travel to Englewood with the sick youngster.

Around 9:30pm, Charles Sr. heard a strange noise he believed to be coming from the kitchen. It sounded like wood cracking, and he presumed the crate of oranges in his kitchen had fallen from a table.

When he got up about a half hour later he noticed that the crate was still in tact so he sent Gow to check on Charles Jr. to make sure it hadn't been coming from his room above the kitchen. When Gow opened the baby's bedroom door, she was shocked to see the crib empty.

Gow immediately ran to get Charles Sr., who found a ransom note on the window sill during a search of the room. He grabbed his gun and searched the surrounding property for intruders, but found no one and no sign of his first-born son. Only twenty minutes after discovering Charles Jr. was missing, local police were on the scene, along with a frenzy-storm of reporters and the family's lawyer.

America was in a state of shock when the Lindbergh baby was reported missing. There was a sense of disbelief that this extraordinary royal prince figure could have been stolen. With no eye-witnesses and few clues except for a homemade ladder left by the kidnappers, the police had a difficult time reconstructing the events of the crime.

What emerged as facts were these:

Sometime between 8-10pm on Tuesday, March 1, 1932, one or more individuals came to the Lindbergh house with a homemade ladder that left scrape marks on the wall to the right of the abby's bedroom window. The kidnappers apparently climbed the ladder and entered the bedroom through the unlocked window. Once inside, they snatched the sleeping baby from the crib. They may have silenced him or rendered him unconscious because no one in the household reported hearing Charlie cry out or struggle as he was taken from his bedroom and whisked away.

The kidnappers left the ladder by a service road and used their car to make a getaway. They had placed a ransom note on the baby's windowsill demanding $50,000 for his safe return and warned Lindbergh there would be trouble if he involved the police. The ransom note was also riddled with spelling mistakes and grammatical irregularities that suggested the person who wrote it did not have a fluent grasp on the English language.

Other than these few facts, the New Jersey State Police, who were now in charge of handling the investigation, had little to go on and only a vague idea of where to start.

Chapter Two

Initially, Charles and Anne Lindbergh were hopeful that they would have their young son returned to them safe and sound. The kidnappers wanted $50,000 and the Lindberghs had it. Together with New Jersey officials, the Lindberghs decided to make it even more tempting for their son's kidnappers to return the young child to his parents by offering a $75,000 reward for the return of Charles Jr. No questions asked. They were surprised when they weren't taken up on their offer.

The kidnappers sent the Lindberghs a second ransom letter in the mail on March 6. The letter was confirmed to be from the same source as the first as both were marked with a distinctive image. In this note, the kidnappers demanded $70,000 in ransom money, and for John Condon to act as an intermediary between the two parties.

While the Lindberghs saw this as a sign of hope, officers were not as sure. It had occurred to them previously that caring for a toddler required a lot of planning from criminals—they would have had to find a place to take care of the young boy and would have had to have bought a number of supplies including food, clothes, and diapers. It would have been much easier on the men to kill the young child after kidnapping him, collect the ransom money, and then disappear before they could be caught. The police warned the Lindberghs against handing over their money without proof that the child was really with the kidnappers, but the Lindberghs had little choice but to cooperate with the kidnapper's demands and hope for the best.

John Condon was chosen as an intermediary between the Lindberghs and the kidnappers who allegedly had their son for several reasons. He was a well known figure in the Bronx at the time, and he had personally offered up $1,000 to the kidnappers if they returned the child safely to a nearby church. Condon received a letter he claimed was from the kidnappers, which Lindbergh believed to be genuine.

Condon arranged to meet the kidnappers to hand over the ransom money during the night. They met at the Woodlawn Cemetery in the Bronx. Condon handed over the money to a man Condon said was named *John*. The man accepted the money, only $50,000, and gave

Condon a note describing where the Lindberghs would be able to find their son alive and well.

Unfortunately, although the Lindberghs followed each of the kidnapper's instructions word for word, they were never reunited with their infant son Charles Lindbergh Jr.

It takes too much planning and resources to care for a toddler. It's much easier to kill the child, pretend he's still alive, collect the ransom, and then immediately skip town. And that is exactly what the kidnappers in the Lindbergh case did.

Two weeks after the $50,000 ransom was delivered, a truck driver walking through the woods stumbled upon the decomposing remains of Charlie less than five miles from his home. From the state of the corpse it appeared he died the very night of the kidnapping. An entire nation mourned Charlie's death as if his death had been one of their very own.

The baby had a fractured skull, and when police found cracks in the ladder, they theorized the breaking ladder startled the kidnapper who then dropped the baby by accident. But many modern investigators disagree with this scenario.

While this theory does explain some of the injuries, it fails to explain all of them. On the left side of the child's head there was a fracture line extending from the soft spot in the top of his skull all the way to the back of his ear. On the right side there was a rounded half-inch diameter defect behind the right ear. While the first injury could be attributed to many scenarios, including being drop from a two-storey tall ladder, the second injury on the right side complicates things more.

Police reports stated that an officer who had been trying to extricate the baby's remains accidentally poked a hole in the side of the skull with a stick, which created the round impact-like injury on the right side. But again, many are skeptical. An individual prodding a body with a stick could not poke a hole through bone with a stick under any circumstance.

There is one possible scenario that could have caused the significant damage to both sides of the skull, and it is anything but accidental—it's murder.

If he was laying on his left side face down on a hard surface and then struck a forceful blow on the right side of the head by a hammer or pipe, that would compress the head. If it was done with sufficient force, the blow could have easily caused the fracturing on the left side.

This theory supports the common idea that the kidnappers killed Charlie intentionally. It also explains how the kidnapper would have been able to keep Charlie quiet while removing him from his room. Most importantly, this theory tells us more about the individuals who could have committed the crime.

Chapter Three

Committing the kidnapping and murder of America's young prince meant automatic death if caught. The individuals who were daring enough to pull this off knew this, and felt confident enough in their skills that they could pull this off and get away with it. They were not first time criminals—they knew what they were doing because they have done it before. They had to have been a career criminal; someone who has spent their life committing crimes. Possibly one who has a pretty good track record of breaking and entering and getting away with it.

It took police two-and-a-half-years to finally corall a suspect due to a combination of foresight and luck. When authorities prepared the original ransom money, they provided nearby banks and stores with lists of the serial numbers of the notes. They also used gold certificates, a currency that was to be discontinued within the year. The idea with this was that the serial numbers on these old bills would be more distinct and therefore easier for merchants and bank tellers to spot.

Two-and-a-half-years after the kidnapping, a german immigrant pulled up to a gas station in New York and bought about 98 cents worth of gas. He payed with a $10 gold certificate. The gas attendant was immediately suspicious—not that he was receiving Lindbergh ransom money, but that America had been off the gold standard for about a year at this point and the bank may not accept the old bill. Just in case this happened when the attendant went to deposit the bill, he wrote down the man's license plate number on the edge of the bill. It belonged to Richard Hauptmann.

When the gold certificate bill used by Richard Hauptmann was brought to the bank, the tellers instantly realized the bill may have been Lindbergh ransom money, and they called the police. Police instantly followed up with the new lead by visiting Hauptmann at his home. Once there, police found a total of $14,000 in gold certificate notes, all of which matched the serial numbers of the Lindbergh ransom money. Hauptmann was arrested on the spot.

On January 3, 1935, Hauptmann went on trial for his participation in the kidnap and murder of Charles Lindbergh Jr. At his trial, Hauptmann presented himself as a hardworking business man who could never have committed such a heinous crime. But a closer look at his background called this assertion into question.

Prior to coming to the United States, Hauptmann had built up an extensive criminal history in Germany. In one of his past offences, Hauptmann had used a ladder to climb into the second story window of a mayor's house to steal a large amount of money, expensive watches, and other valuables. In another, Hauptmann worked with an accomplice to hold up and rob a woman pushing her baby carriage down the road at gunpoint.

To get to the United States, Hauptmann had to escape from jail, stow away on a steamship, and lie his way through American immigration. So despite his clean, businessman demeanour Hauptmann was bold, ruthless, and criminally sophisticated—the very attributes modern profilers associate with the person who must have committed the Lindbergh Baby murder. Not to mention his history of using ladders to commit crimes.

Prosecutors claimed that Hauptmann personally built the kidnap ladder, but Hauptmann denied ever seeing it. The ladder itself would have been difficult to make. It was made of scrap materials; whoever constructed the ladder used whatever they could scrounge up to build it. It was cleverly designed with three sections that nestled together. This design made it easier to store, set up, and move because it was able to collapse to a small size.

After the kidnapping, the police brought the ladder to Arthur Kailer, a wood expert, to see if he could find clues that would lead to the kidnapper. Kailer numbered every piece of wood and traced their origins. When it came to Hauptmann's trial, the most important piece of the ladder was rail 16, which was positively identified as coming from the floorboards in Hauptmann's attic by Kailer thanks to the matching grain patterns on both pieces of wood.

Hauptmann's trial was six weeks of gruelling testimony that came to a conclusion on Feb 13, 1935 when the jury handed down its verdict. Guilty as charged. The sentence? Death.

Chapter Four

While most people believe Hauptmann indefinitely participated in the crime, many have speculated that Hauptmann likely didn't act alone. As he waited in his cell for his death, prosecutors offered him a deal. They would spare his life if he named his accomplices. Hauptmann was a stubborn man though. He was determined to die declaring himself innocent, and therefore never revealed anything to the court. His fate was sealed. He was executed by electric chair on April 3, 1936 at the age of 36.

Because he chose to die when he could've saved his own life, many began to wonder if Hauptmann might have been innocent after all. Hauptmann's claims of innocence was seconded by his wife, Anna Schoeffler, who was now left to raise their young son alone. An outpouring of support for Schoeffler and her convicted husband especially came from Hauptmann's hometown of Kamenz, Germany.

There are three definitive scenarios surrounding Hauptmann's guilt in the case: that Hauptmann is innocent, that Hauptmann is guilty and he acted alone, and finally that Hauptmann is guilty but he acted with accomplices.

The most popular theory in modern days is that Hauptmann was in fact guilty, but that he acted with accomplices—a theory that goes in line with what the prosecutors at Hauptmann's trial themselves believed.

One reason for this speculation is the ransom money. Only one third of the ransom money was ever discovered, and it was discovered hidden away in Hauptmann's home. Perhaps the other two thirds are with two accomplices.

The second reason has to do with the psychological profile of the case. Generally with kidnapping cases, the perpetrator of the crime relies on others involved to convince themselves into committing the crime. They need constant reminders and support in order to go through with the act, especially if they're victimizing someone that feels personal to themselves. Hauptmann would have needed a lot of goading and reminders so that kidnapping and killing the Lindbergh's boy would feel normal. Especially since he had a young boy at home himself.

The third reason has to do with the logistics of the crime. The night of the kidnapping, it was dark and dreary out. The ground was muddy and wet, making it very slippery. Committing the crime alone would have been risky, as the chance for injury and mistake was so high. If accomplices were involved, they would've been able to help hold the ladder, do the surveillance, and help with the getaway. Without extra help with these tasks, kidnapping the Lindbergh baby would have been almost impossible.

Whether it was two, three or more people involved that night remains to be unseen. What is fairly certain though, is that it was not one person acting alone.

No suspects other than Hauptmann have ever been identified. Once Hauptmann was arrested, the investigation into the kidnapping of Charles Lindbergh Jr was shut down. It had been a long two-year investigation for the police, which had been full of pressures and media attention. They wanted it to be over. It had to end.

Modern investigators love looking back at the Lindbergh kidnapping case. While there was a definite conclusion to the original investigation, there were just enough questions left unanswered to leave a shade of mystery over the full truth.

Other suspects or potential accomplices have been identified since the Lindbergh kidnapping case was filed officially as closed. One popular alternative explanation for the kidnapping is that whoever took Charles Jr. that night was from inside the house itself, or at least had ties to the family.

Following this train of thought, Dwight Morrow Jr., Charles Lindbergh's brother-in-law, is a common suspect. Morrow would have known that the Lindberghs were staying in Hopewell, not Englewood as usual, that night. He also would have known exactly where in the house Charlie slept and what time he was normally put down for the night and check on later.

Dwight Morrow Jr. was not as successful as his sister and her famous husband, and it is likely that he could've used the kidnapping as means to get a piece of the family's wealth. Charles Lindbergh himself is also brought up as a suspect, possibly working with his brother-in-law or another accomplice who was able to kidnap the child while Charles spent time with his family, giving him a perfect alibi.

Charles Lindbergh Sr. seemingly would have had no need to kidnap his child, but many believe that the family may have recently found out that their son was handicapped physically. Not wanting to raise the child himself, Lindbergh was having arrangements be made secretly for the young boy to be raised in Germany instead. The ransom money was for services paid. In this scenario, it is believed that Lindbergh believed his child was still alive until his small, decomposing body was found less than five miles away from the family's Hopewell home.

Chapter Five

After the investigation into their son's kidnapping was concluded, the Lindbergh family was forced into a brief period of self-exile in Europe. The normally intensely private family became exasperated by the unrelenting public attention they had received. They felt like they had no time to grieve in private and peace for their young son.

On top of seeking privacy, the family also decided to move in an effort to protect their family. After Charles Lindbergh Jr.'s disappearance and death, Anne and Charles Sr. had had another son, Jon Lindbergh. They were petrified their son, who was born in 1932, would become an easy target as the family was in the media so much.

Before the sun came out to rise on December 22, 1935, the family of three set foot as the only passengers aboard the SS *American Importer*. They were headed for Liverpool.

The family completed this move under complete secrecy. They had been issued diplomatic passports and used these to travel under false names. The Lindberghs had been safely away at sea for days before their unannounced departure was reported on in America.

For the next three years, Anne and Charles Lindbergh traveled and lived all across Europe until 1939, when they returned home to America. The Lindbergh family had grown since they left—the couple now had five children. They were a picture of happiness.

Unfortunately, Lindbergh's career never again reached the soaring heights it had before his son's death. In 1940, Lindbergh became the spokesman for the anti-war *America First* committee. Lindbergh was outspoken on his views that America should have been fighting to strike a neutrality pact with Germany in order to side with the aggressive country that had Hitler at its reigns. And while Lindbergh criticized Hitler's anti-Semitic views, he adopted the Nazi view that ensuring the continuation of the *White Race* in Europe was more of a priority than ensuring the continuation of democracy across the continent.

The tarnishing of Charles Lindbergh's reputation continued after his death. Thirty years after Lindbergh's death, and two-and-a-half after his widow's, the Lindbergh children and the public learned that Charles had been maintaining three secret families across Europe. These families included seven out-of-wedlock children by three separate women. This image of Charles was shockingly far from the man who had only ever asked one woman out on a date in his lifetime—his later-wife Anne Morrow.

Lindbergh's life of secret families began in 1957 when he established a romantic relationship with a German woman by the name of Brigitte Hesshaimer. Hesshaimer bore Lindbergh three children. Later, Lindbergh fathered two more children with Hesshaimer's sister Mariette Hesshaimer, and another two children with his private secretary in Europe who went by the name of Valeska. Lindbergh wrote letters to all three women ten days before he died begging the women to maintain their secret connections after his death.

Chapter Six

The Lindbergh family was once the perfect picture of the American dream. They had it all. Until March 1, 1932, when everything they loved, their young son Charles Jr., was taken from them. If having their son kidnapped and killed wasn't enough, the media circus that was built up around the family forced them out of their home and country.

After self-exiling to Europe, the family found peace. They moved on from the crime that haunted their past in order to enjoy the lives they had ahead of them with their five other children.

Charles Lindbergh never fully recovered, though. He was a broken man without his reputation, his home, and his first-born son.

The Lindbergh's were once the perfect example of the American dream. Now, they remain the perfect example of how the loss of a child never really leaves the hearts of the grieving parents, and of how that grief can destroy all it touches.

MISTY COPSEY

Misty Copsey was fourteen years old when she disappeared on September 17th, 1992 after a trip to the Puyallup Fair.

Her case remains a showcase of administrative screw-ups and dropped balls. She was initially thought of as a runaway before foul play was finally suspected a month after the fact. Subsequently, there have been at least five people suspected of committing her abduction.

But the Puyallup police did not get within sniffing distance of Misty or charging anyone with her disappearance. Three different police chiefs and numerous detectives all took a swing at the case and whiffed. No one in law enforcement has been able to answer the question on everyone's lips.

What happened to Misty Copsey?

A GOOD GIRL

Misty was born in 1978 to Diana and Paul "Buck" Copsey. Her father was a firefighter but the couple split up shortly after she was born and Misty lived with her mother.

Misty got good grades in school, excelling particularly in Math. During her last quarter at Spanaway Lake Junior High School, she got A's and B's. Athletic, she played softball, volleyball, and basketball before breaking both forearms during an athletic practice.

Misty was not the ringleader of a bad crowd. She was diffident but funny, entertaining her friends while skipping around and singing the theme song to Sesame Street.

She did not have much in regards to material wants. Her mother eked out a living as an in-home care nurse and they lived in a mobile home park until she was fourteen. Seeking a better place to live, Diana and Misty moved into a duplex where she now had her own room. But

Misty longed for her friend who lived in and around the old trailer park. She would make it back there when she could to just hang out.

Tall, blonde and with green eyes, Misty was cute enough to draw the attention of boys. She remained chaste, however, and was not dating like so many of her other friends.

Her innocent, girl-next-door looks would draw the attention of Rheuban Schmidt. Rheuban looked like a casting call actor for a meth head. He sported a reverse mullet, a hairstyle that was cut close to the sides with curls on top. He had beady, green eyes that screamed low IQ. One of Misty's friends described him as a "scuzzy looking dude" but he nonetheless befriends Misty, much to the chagrin of her mother.

Diana grew suspicious of the relationship as Rheuban was four years older and a high school dropout. On one occasion, she listened in on the other end of a phone conversation Misty was having with Rheuban.

"I get horny just looking at you, Misty," Rheuban said, whispering like an old pervert.

Diana became enraged and ordered her daughter off the phone.

"Don't ever talk to that idiot again...."

ENTER CORY BOBER

Cory Bober was a thorn in the side of police every since the Green River killings became a national news story. He would insist that the police are "incompetent fools" while organizing his own searches for her remains. Diana would later accuse him of killing her daughter but he would respond by telling Diana that she was being "ungrateful." He was, after all, the only man on the case.

Bober was a recluse without a vehicle or a drive's license. An inveterate marijuana user, he had a record for both possession and dealing. He was also obsessed with cases of murdered or slain women in his home state of Washington. He had a stack of binders with autopsy reports, pictures, and other arcane details.

Bober came under the radar of the police in Puyallup when he became obsessed with the Green River Killer case. He had a brief acquaintance with Randall Dean Achziger, remembering a conversation where the man told him that the killer inserted rocks into the remains of his victim. Bober became suspicious as that would turn out to be a piece of information only known to police. He then went on a one-man crusade to prove the guilt of Achziger. Bober would interview his ex-girlfriends, friends, co-workers and present all of this in an affidavit to the courts.

Achziger found it ridiculous and annoying.

So did the police.

The Green River Killer would turn out to be a painter named Gary Leon Ridgway.

Bober didn't give up, however. He knew Achziger was the guy.

Bober had his own theories about who was performing the killings. Some were wild and outlandish conspiracy theories. Others were spot on. He would notice that there were victims that "had disappeared on the very same date that others were discovered. Some victims seemed to almost 'commemorate' the deaths or discoveries of others; one would die on a particular date and another would disappear a year to the day later on the very same date."

The police dismissed his theories as the rantings of a crack head. But Bober would be willing to show the proof of his connect the dots calculations. He pointed to the cases of Kim Delange, a 15-year-old killed in 1988 and Anna Chebetnoy, a 14-year-old killed in 1990. Both of their bodies would be found along Highway 410, east of Enumclaw.

Bober discovered that the remains of both girls were found in the same section of 410. The girls were found two years and one month apart. He felt that the killer was following a pattern.

He called the police department and left a voice mail. He predicted that a teen girl from Puyallup would disappear and her remains would be found on Highway 410 in the same vicinity where the other girl's bodies were found. Bober gave him the name of the man whom he felt was the serial killer.

Randall Achziger.

But the police were now used to his calls and viewed him as a crank. A nutcake with a strange vendetta.

His prediction would be half-right, however.

There would be no body found on Highway 410.

But a teenage girl would disappear.

Her name was Misty Copsey.

A NIGHT AT THE FAIR

On September 17th, 1992, Diana told her daughter Misty and her best friend Trina Bevard to behave themselves. Misty had convinced her mother to let them stay out that night...free of any meddlesome adults. But Trina's guardian would not allow her to go without an adult driving them home.

Diana worked as a caregiver for a 97-year-old Alzheimer patient who could not be left alone. She would not be able to drive the girls home. But Misty checked the bus schedules and convinced her mother that they would be okay. There was a bus that left the fair at 8:40 p.m.

Misty then convinced her mother to lie to Trina's guardian, Marlene Shoemaker.

"No worries," Diana said to Marlene. "I'll bring them home."

She wanted to be the cool parent, different from the stuffy adults who forgot what it was like to be fourteen. If it meant telling a white lie so her little girl could have some happiness, so be it.

What was the worst that could happen?

Diana dropped the girls off and gave them one last warning.

"Get home safe."

It would be the last time she would ever see her daughter again.

THE PHONE CALL

A few hours later, Diana would then receive a phone call from Misty as she tended to her elderly patient. Misty told her that she had missed the bus but could get a ride from Rheuban Schmidt.

Diana, knowing what kind of unsavory character Schmidt was, adamantly refused. She told Misty to find someone else to give her a ride back. Misty had an electronic diary which she used to store phone numbers. She told her mother she would find someone trustworthy to call for a ride.

"You call me back when you find someone," Diana said.

"I will. I promise."

Diana would wait all night for the phone call.

In the ensuing hours, Misty would not call back.

Worried, Diane called home in the hope that Misty had gotten a ride without calling her.

No answer.

Diana didn't panic. She figured that Misty went home with that scumbag Schmidt and didn't want to get yelled out for disobeying her.

She's going to get yelled at either/or. All Diana wanted was for her daughter to be safe.

Her shift finally ended and Diana drove back home in a rush.

Upon entering her house, she called out for Misty.

Silence.

She went into Misty's room and saw that it had been untouched from the previous night.

Diana would call the police in a panic. She told them that her daughter had not come home from the fair. The dispatcher would tell her that the police could not do anything about it for thirty days as it "sounded like a runaway case."

Diana knew otherwise.

Trying to calm herself, she figured that Misty was with Trina, that the two of them would be okay.

She called Trina's home.

No answer.

She then began scorching the earth with phone calls.

She would call Rheuban but he told her that she called but he didn't have the gas to go get her. She then called numerous friends of Misty and her mother.

No one had seen Misty.

She called Trina's home again, got no answer, then drove out to her house. She then went to the police department and filed a formal report with the Pierce County's Sheriff's Department who handled runaways as opposed to the Puyallup Police.

MISTY'S MISSING

Misty's friend Trina called Diana after she came back from school. She told the frantic mother that she didn't know where Misty was.

"The last time I saw her, she was heading for the bus," she said.

Diana would call Rheuban again. She would get his roommate this time, James Tinsley.

Diana needed answers. She interrogated the young fifteen-year-old like a grizzled police detective. She asked if Rheuban had been home all night. James then told her that Rheuban and his uncle went to pick up Misty but that he wasn't home just yet.

Later, Diana would call back and Rheuban would tell her that his roommate got the story wrong. He went to a party instead and didn't pick up Misty. He didn't know where she was.

Diana pleaded for the police to do something. They dragged their heels and began talking to some of Misty's friends. "Just call if she calls," they informed them. "No one gets in trouble."

Diana printed fliers with Misty's picture. She plastered them in and around the fairgrounds while calling the media.

The one woman search team would yield no leads. Rheuban would stop by and ask if the police had found anything yet. Diana would then wait at the bus stop near the fairgrounds to inquire with different drivers on the route. She found one driver who said that he saw Misty. She had asked when the next bus to Spanaway was arriving. The driver said it wasn't and that he was done for the night. He gave her instructions on which bus to take but she walked away before he could complete his sentence.

AN ERROR OF JUDGEMENT

Among the many mistakes that the Puyallup police made in the investigation of Misty's disappearance was to make the assumption that she was a runaway. Why they didn't entertain the prospect that she could have been kidnapped and murdered gave the abductor precious time to cover his tracks.

The police came to this erroneous conclusion after they interviewed Misty's mother, Diana. They thought she was a liar and an alcoholic. They then interviewed a pair of Misty's classmates who really didn't know her that well or accompany her to the fair.

A series of cover-ups then ensued, as the police told the media Misty had been found (where they got that information remains a mystery) and made no further investigation.

Until Diana and the media started to make a fuss. The department had to save face and eventually one of the detectives believed that this was not a runaway case.

Misty's disappearance could not be ignored any longer.

Police would talk to the various fair workers and security guards. No one had recalled seeing Misty.

The police then turned to her family, interviewing and doing background checks on both Misty's father, Buck, and Diana.

Their impressions of the duo would support their initial theory that Misty runaway. Diana was an alcoholic with multiple DUIs and seven years prior she had been convicted of welfare fraud. Buck confirmed that his daughter and Diana would have their issues.

Carver then discovered that Diana had filed a runaway report on Misty a month prior to her disappearing.

Diana would later state that the report was wrong. She thought Misty had disappeared then found her in the bedroom. She was too ashamed to tell the police it had been a false alarm.

With the police questioning and media coverage, Misty Copsey was now the talk of her Spanaway Lake Junior High school.

Rumors would abound at the school, one of which came from Misty Matthews who said that Misty had called her from Olympia. Another student stated that she saw Misty at a Color Me Badd concert at the fair.

The rumors were enough to prompt Carver to remove Misty from the FBI's National Crime Information Center as a missing person. He would once again treat her as a runaway.

BOBER'S THEORY

Cory Bober's knew he was right. He knew that police would find a body of a young woman off Highway 410.

He waited but nothing happened.

Until his mother showed him the flier of Misty's disappearance.

Right again!

Heart racing, he called the number on the flier. Bober would get into contact with Diana and hurriedly told her all about his research.

He talked about the Green River Killer, where and how he killed his victims. He would tell Diana that her disappearance was connected to the same guy responsible for the murdered Puyallup Girls, Kim Delange and Anne Chebetnoy.

Cory would apologize to Diana because he knew that Misty was dead. He predicted her body would be found somewhere along Highway 410.

The two would form an uneasy alliance. Bober became Misty's personal avenger. He would start a phone/letter/media campaign to prove the police wrong and himself right.

Misty was no runaway.

She was a victim of Randall Achziger.

In October, however, Bober would be arrested for selling marijuana. He was then accosted by Sgt.Herm Carver who tired of the young man meddling in police affairs.

"He walked in the room I was being held in – looking tired and pissed off. He said, 'I got out of bed tonight, and came down here to meet you – just to see what kind of a hypocrite you REALLY ARE!'

I said (being cocky), 'It's not MY FAULT – HERM – that you don't believe Misty Copsey's MISSING!!'

He yelled (angry), 'DON'T YOU EVER CALL ME BY MY FIRST NAME – IT'S SGT. CARVER TO YOU!!!'"

Bober's journals, November 1992

THIRTY DAYS MISSING

Sgt. Herm Carver and Deputy Brian Coburn would each individually warn Diana of the troublemaker that Bober was. Still, the worried mother would welcome his assistance as she needed all the help she could get. After numerous phone calls, the two would finally meet after a month of Misty being missing. Diana had nowhere else to turn but to the shaggy-haired twenty-six-year-old who lived with his parents.

The police were going through the motions on their end. Carver reactivated Misty's name on state and national lists but only because he was legally required to do so. At this point, he still believed Misty to be a runaway and doubted Diana's veracity.

Meanwhile, Diana would find Cory Bober's constant badgering to be annoying. It got so bad she filed a restraining order against him.

"My daughter has been missing for six weeks from the Puyallup Fair," Diana wrote in the restraining order. "Cory Bober has called me on a daily basis, telling me my daughter is dead. I was advised by Deputy Brian Coburn to file this complaint if I felt threatened."

The order would only last two weeks. Diana would then call the courts and rescind her request. She would later call Bober and apologize. Her daughter had been missing for over 56 days. Bober was annoying as hell but he was the only one doing research. The only one who cared.

Bober organized a volunteer search for Misty in the Green River area. He somehow coerced someone on the police forensic team to tell him the general vicinity of where one of the Puyallup girl's body was found. Bober surmised that Misty's body would be found in the same general area.

Seventy-two days after Misty had gone missing, there was now a volunteer team searching for her.

Nothing came out of the search.

But Diana would later spot Rheuban at a grocery store and confront him. The young man ran and got into a truck with an older man. She saw the look of fear and apprehension on both men as they sped off.

Diana would then lapse into a depression. She tried to commit suicide with booze and prescription drugs.

The next day she would wake up in a hospital. She would spend the next day there, drying out until being discharged back into the nightmare that had become her life.

A PLEA TO THE PUBLIC

Four months after Misty's disappearance, Diana would appear on a local TV station for a special on the Green River Killer. Jim Doyon, the homicide detective who worked the case, spoke of the killings but deferred on stating if Delange and Chebetnoy(the slain Puyallup girls) were connected.

Doyon took an interest in Misty's case. He would journey to Highway 410 and search near milepost 30 where the bodies of Delange and Chebetnoy had been discovered.

Like Bober and the volunteer search team, he too came up empty.

Bober was undaunted and organized another search. He realized that they had been searching in the wrong spot. They were searching on the south side of the highway when the should have been searching on the north.

Twelve people would show up for the search. Diana would arrive with her older sister, Debra. Bober would arrive with Al Hensley, the father of one of the slain Puyallup girls along with his 14-year old Boy Scout nephew, Jaremy Brown.

It would be the Boy Scout that would make the find

Poking into a ditch with his stick, he saw the crumpled blue jeans. Socks fell out of the jeans.

Baggy and stone-washed, they were cuffed at the bottom. The same jeans that Misty had borrowed from her mother on the night of the fair. The jeans were too big for her and Diana remembered them cuffing them on the bottom.

Bober became excited. He knew that the killer had planted the jeans there as a taunt.

He was right. The police were wrong.

But Diana, according to her sister, "broke into a million pieces."

THE KILLING FIELD

Seven dead women had been found in the nine-mile stretch between Enumclaw and Greenwater in the eight years prior to Misty's disappearance.

The two slain Puyallup girls were found in the same area in 1988 and 1991, only one hundred feet apart. They were left off a footpath that had been hidden by thick brush.

Both of the teenage girls had been presumed abducted from the Puyallup shopping center. Detective Jim Doyon believed privately that the cases were connected. He arrived at the site where Misty's jeans were found and interviewed witnesses, particularly Diana and Bober.

The jeans were taken to the lab and the forensic analysis indicated that the jeans had been in the ditch for some time.

Police suspected that someone (Bober? Diana?) had planted the jeans there.

What was undeniable that the jeans were found only a ten minute walk away from where the bodies of the two slain Puyallup girls were found.

SUSPICIONS ARISE

People began to talk. There were reporters who believed the jeans were planted there. Some were talking as if Diana and Bober were lovers and had plotted this for some insurance money.

Dede Miles, a fifteen-year-old friend of Misty, would come to Sgt. Carver with a tip. She said there was a boy that kept coming over to Misty's parties. He would always leave before her mother came home.

His name was Rheuban Schmidt.

Finally, the unkempt looking young man would come under the radar of the police.

Diana, meanwhile, began to suspect Cory Bober.

How did he know where to look? Why was this stranger so interested in the case to begin with? How did he know so much?

The police had warned her to stay away from him. Now she felt compelled to tell the police of her suspicions.

"Diana comes to station. Now feels Cory Bober may be involved in Misty's disappearance. I asked Diana to submit a written statement to that effect and why she feels he may be involved – she agreed to do so."

Carver's notes

AN INTERVIEW WITH TRINA

Detective Jim Doyon would interview the fifteen-year-old Trina Bevard, the last person to see Misty alive.

Six months had passed. Doyon had brought along the jeans with him, the sight of which made Trina cry.

"It seems to me like something that Misty was wearing that night," Trina said. "It looks very close to what Misty was wearing. The socks, they match what she was wearing. The jeans are big, so – her jeans were baggy that night, that she was wearing. They're – they were light blue like they are in the photo. It just seems, you know, it was the clothes that she was wearing."

Doyon would go on to ask what she was wearing (a pullover) and if she had any jewelry. He then asked if she had any cigarettes or birth control pills.

"No," Trina said. "She was straight. She was a virgin. She didn't smoke, she didn't drink, she didn't do drugs. She was clean, so she had no reason to do anything. She wasn't sexually active."

Trina then revealed that the girls made five calls to Rheuban. They could not get a hold of him. They finally got him on the line and he still refused to pick them up even when the girls offered him money. Misty told him about a key under the front doormat of her home. He could go inside, get money for gas and come pick them up.

Trina stated that she didn't trust Rheuban but only because he didn't keep his word and come pick them up. She then called a 23-year old friend named Mike Rhyner for a ride but they got disconnected. The girls were then stranded. They walked downtown to get to the bus stop before spotting a phone booth by a convenience store. Misty then called her mother, telling her that if Rheuban didn't come pick her up she would take the bus. The two argued as Diana didn't want Misty around Rheuban.

Trina had to get home by 10 p.m. She had about an hour and a half to get home which wasn't that far. Misty could not walk the ten miles to Spanaway.

Trina then decided to walk. She gave Misty her extra money for the bus.

"At that time I made my decision of walking home and she said she would take the bus," Trina recalled. "The last words that I said to her were 'Be careful,' and she turned around and told me the same and we walked off in different directions"

Trina also dismissed the notion of Misty being a runaway.

" Her mom just bought her a stereo and she was so excited and she went shopping and she got new clothes,"Trina recalled. She was telling me all about it. She was really excited about it.

BOBER GOES TO JAIL

Meanwhile, Bober would be sentenced to fourteen months in prison for the marijuana possession. He felt that the sentencing was too punitive and threatened law enforcement that they would never find Misty without him. His fellow inmates thought he was crazy and began calling him "snitch" and "The Green River Killer".

Jail would not slow down Bober's efforts, however. He continued to research and write Misty's mother.

"Dear Diana,

...When we found Misty's clothes, part of me died and I watched a part of you die too (much more than a "part") and I was at a total loss for words. I never wanted to be the one to show you your most horrible fears were true and that your daughter is truly dead at the hands of a sick murderer. I will never rest until the killer (Randy Achziger) is brought to justice and dead, if it takes my life to do it."

AMERICA'S MOST WANTED

Misty's case would eventually be broadcast nationally as it was featured on the America's Most Wanted television show.

Over twenty-eight tips came into Sgt. Carver from people who watched the broadcast.

When the tips went nowhere, Diana's suspicions returned to her original suspect, Rheuban Schmidt. She wanted Carver to speak to the young man but the Sergeant would take a circuitous route to get to Schmidt.

Carver would speak to Frank Rodriguez, the owner of Adam's Ribs, a restaurant where Rheuban worked. He convinced the owner to try and find out how much Rheuban knew about Misty.

"3-4-93 @ 1500: Frank states Rheuban said the following during a lengthy conversation about Misty Copsey:

- Yeah, I know about it.

- I know exactly where she is buried.

- They found the clothes but she is buried 6 miles from there.

- They're off by 6 or 6 1/2 miles."

— Excerpt from Carver's notes

Carver would then wait for Rheuban outside the restaurant before his shift started. Schmidt arrived, saw the cops and immediately ran off. The detectives would eventually catch up with him.

Rheuban would concede that he had received calls from Misty the night of her disappearance. But his story corroborated with Trina's, he told the girls he had no gas and could not pick them up.

Carver then asked if he knew where Misty was buried but Rheuban was adamant that he "said those things to get Frank off my back."

Rheuban then revealed that he suffered from "black outs". He stated that he did not recall anything until the daylight hours of September 18th, 1992.

The detectives pounced, asking if it was possible that he blacked out, picked up Misty and harmed her.

Rheuban claimed he didn't know.

All he knew was that he drove out to his grandmother's farmhouse and couldn't recall why.

Detectives would then give Rheuban a polygraph test.

They would later state that the suspect "zoned out" during the test, nearly falling asleep. The tests were inconclusive but detectives felt as if he were trying to beat the test.

A LITTLE LIE

Rheuban fell off the detective's radar when Carver talked to Dede Miles again. Dede would tell the detective that Trina had not walked home from the fairground like she told him.

Dede said that Trina had a boyfriend come pick her up and didn't want anyone to know.

Trina's boyfriend's name was Michael J. Rhyner. He had nothing on his record aside from traffic stops but he had friends that were connected with Chebetnoy and Delange.

He also had a complaint when he was sixteen years old. He was accused of an abduction rape wherein he used a knife and a cigarette lighter to terrorize an eleven-year-old.

Charges were never filed for an undisclosed reason.

Carver brought Trina in for more questioning. He wanted the truth. The truth about who picked her up that night. The truth about Misty.

But the truth was that Trina told the Sgt. Carver and Detective Tom Matison that she lied because she feared "getting into trouble with her guardian about it."

Trina admitted that she called Rhyner, got disconnected and left a message. She told Misty that they could both ride with Rhyner but Misty said no.

"Trina would not be specific why Misty did not trust Rhyner, but the indication was that Rhyner might have 'come on' to Misty at one time and she did not like it. Trina states that she and Rhyner are friends, but not involved."

— Matison's notes

Trina said that she started to walk and then Rhyner picked her up and dropped her off. The detectives asked if perhaps Rhyner had picked up Misty but she said no.

FRANK RODRIGUEZ' FOLLOW UP

Diana would state that Frank Rodriguez, Rheuban's employer, would call her to say that Rheuban had "bragged about doing something" to Misty with his uncle. Frank didn't fully believe him, however, as Rheuban was "weird" and always bragging about stuff he didn't do.

Diana then approached Carver about Rheuban and the sergeant went ballistic.

"We have our man!" he said.

The man he sought was Michael Rhyner, Trina Bevard's boyfriend.

"We share our knowledge of Mike Rhyner and how he is involved with Misty and Trina – and the fact Trina lied to Doyon. We state that there is an excellent possibility that Rhyner may be linked to Chebetnoy and DeLange. Exchange of information is extremely beneficial."

— Carver's notes

"Sgt. Carver believes that Rhyner dropped Bevard off, returned to the area of the fairgrounds, located Misty Copsey, convinced her to get into his vehicle and drove off with her."

— Doyon's notes

Police set up a sting on Rhyner. The car mechanic was selling his 1981 blue Ford Escort for $200 bucks.

The buyer was an undercover cop.

He watched as Rhyner hurriedly took out trash from the car before the sale. The police then did a forensic examination of the car.

Meanwhile, Rheuban's green Nova was being crushed at a wrecking yard. The Puyallup police didn't care as the tweaker was no longer on their radar. Also, Randy Achziger, Bober's suspect, had been charged and convicted for the rape of a seven-year-old.

INTERROGATING RHYNER

Ideally, Detectives Matison and Sgt. Carver wanted the forensics back from Rhyner's Escort before they spoke to him. But the wait became interminable and they brought him in for questioning without some evidence to back up their suspicions.

Rhyner's story would match that of Trina's. He picked Trina up and went back home. He said that he and Trina were only "good friends" and he had met Misty only four times. Matison then asked Rhyner if he felt Misty was alive and what should happen to the person who harmed her.

Rhyner knew what the detective was getting at. On his own volition, Rhyner told the detectives about his juvenile complaint from years ago. He stated he had been cleared and knew that was why they were looking at him now.

"First thing I thought, you know, well, that's in my file," Rhyner said. "Now you guys are going to think I did it since it's in my file. About Misty, that's the one thing that worried me."

Rhyner then passed a polygraph test.

Grasping at straws, the police then turned their sights back on Rheuban. If only they had impounded his car when they had the chance...

TOO LITTLE TOO LATE

"Rheuban Schmidt's initial interview with Sgt. Carver and I created more questions than answers. He was very vague about what he did that September 17th and finally said that he had a 'blackout' and 'woke up' at his grandmother's property near Enumclaw.

...Schmidt had told Frank Rodriguez that Misty's body was six miles from where the jeans were found. He now claims that he said this just to get Rodriguez "off his back," and was not a true statement.

He was driving a Green Chev Nova at the time but he no longer has the vehicle. It was repossessed.

Schmidt also mentioned that his Grandmother's property is located in King County by Buckley and is over a hundred acres. The property has cows on it. Few people enter onto the property."

— Matison's notes

Tinsley, fifteen years old at the time of Misty's disappearance, told police the Rheuban was his roommate for only a few months. He described Rheuban as a short-tempered guy who had a thirteen-year-old girlfriend. The girlfriend, Tinsley said, got jealous when Rheuban got a call from Misty.

Tinsley stated that Rheuban had left the apartment in a huff then came back between eleven and one at night.

So Rheuban did not "black out" as he told detectives. N

"What do you think might have happened to her?" Matison asked.

"Um, I couldn't, I couldn't say because I have no idea," Tinsley said.

"Well, can you speculate?"

"With Rheuban, this is just that I, this, this is what I say with Rheuban because I, I figure that um that he, he tried to, he tried to um, get with her or something and she said, she said no and he got all pissed and did something, I don't know, that's just a second guess."

"You think Rheuban would be capable of ah, kidnapping and killing somebody?"

"I think he could," Tinsley said.

Detectives would meet with Rheuban again, relaying the information that Tinsley recalled him coming back to the apartment that night.

But Rheuban remained adamant in stating that he didn't remember what he did. The detectives then drove him out to his grandmother's farm which had over 100-acres...100 secluded acres.

Detective Matison would note that Rheuban's grandmother's house six miles north of Buckley. Rheuban told Frank that Misty would be buried six miles away from where her jeans were found which would place it in the close vicinity of his grandmother's farm. They would go to inquire with his grandmother but she was not home.

They did not follow-up with the grandmother .

Even so, Rheuban's story no longer held up. He told Misty that he didn't have any gas. He lived sixteen miles away from the fair.

But then he stated that he had driven to his grandmother's farm in Buckley then returned home.

A sixty-mile round trip.

Detectives would give him another polygraph test which he passed.

"It appears that Rheuban Schmidt was not involved in the disappearance of Misty Copsey. He, however, has no alibi as to his movements during the evening of her disappearance, as well as no memory; he claimed that he had a blackout. He acknowledges that he left the residence of James Tinsley, but does not remember what he did.

Investigation to continue."

— Matison's notes

ONE YEAR ANNIVERSARY

The local media ran a few more stories on Misty's disappearance as the Puyallup Fair started. The forensic test on Rhyner's test finally came through. There was no match with Misty anywhere.

Now once again grasping at straws, Carver would turn to Diana and her associates. He would interview Diana's parole officer and one of her ex-boyfriends.

Misty's father, Buck, was asked to take a polygraph test. He gave consent and passed.

"I explained to her that missing person investigations, at some point in time, must eliminate the parents of any wrongdoing. Diana agreed to the examination."

— Carver's notes

Diana would pass her polygraph test but Jim Corey, Doyon's colleague, said that Diana's polygraph would prove to be inconclusive and that perhaps she had something to do with planting the jeans at the location on Hwy 410.

Carver had always had his doubts about Diana and felt that she planted the jeans.

But the leads would eventually dry up. After nine years, Misty Copsey's disappearance would turn cold.

No one was ever charged with her disappearance.

THE AFTERMATH

Diana would hand out fliers at the Puyallup Fairgrounds every year.

She was doing more than law enforcement and even the media.

Every now and then, a local reporter would run a story about Misty. A few cranks would call in and say that they knew something but it would lead to nowhere. Then that would be it. Everything would run dry.

Detective Jim Doyon felt that she was deceased.

BOBER TO THE RESCUE

Bober was then caught for marijuana possession again but this time, he pressed for an advantage. He would gain the Washington State Patrol crime lab report on Misty's jeans, compiled after their 1993 discovery.

He argued that the lab report was part of his defense....he gambled and won.

Obtaining the prized document, the amateur sleuth went to work. The report stated there was no blood, no semen. But there were hairs, fibers, and three red paint chips. There were also holes in the left leg in the jeans, above the knee.

Bober knew that somehow, someway, Randy Achziger was involved. That he killed Misty.

The forensic details raced through Bober's head...red paint chips...red paint chips...

He knew that Bober had a red Porsche. He knew that the paint chips would match.

But the police had another suspect they didn't tell anyone about.

Robert Leslie Hickey.

Hickey's hunting ground was the Puyallup area where he specialized in abduction rapes.

He also drove a red Camaro.

Puyallup police had him on their list as a possible suspect but he was never questioned nor did they obtain forensic samples from his car.

Thirteen years later, however, they would collect samples from Achziger's old car. The car had been sold and the new owner was open to having forensics performed on it.

The particles would be sent to a crime lab which already had a backlog of over a year.

With nothing else left to do, the police turned once again to Rheuban Schmidt.

"I think it's worth taking another shot at Schmidt, and we're planning on it. He's been clean since 1993 ...

— Excerpt from notes by Lt. Dave McDonald, March 19, 2006

Only Schmidt had not been clean. He had been convicted of second-degree theft in 2000. In early 1996, he was accused of rape by one of Misty's best friends. He had held a pillow over her face to silence her but two weeks after filing the report, the girl back away from her accusation and did not file charges.

"[She] told me that she would be undergoing counseling related to the rape, but that she did not want to undergo any additional stress that may be caused by further investigation or possible prosecution in this matter.

Case cleared exceptional/refused by victim."

— Pierce County sheriff's report, Feb. 6, 1996

Later in 2006, Puyallup police gathered more reports on Rheuban. One was a domestic violence protection order requested by his wife, the mother of his three children.

"Rheuban has previously told her that if she ever had him served with a court order he'd 1) burn her house down with her and her kids in it, and 2) send 'some guys' to kick in her door and take money from her.

(She) said Rheuban told her that they'd get money from her if they had to beat her, rape her and then rob her.

(She) said Rheuban told her that if it came to that she 'wouldn't be breathing' when they were done with her."

— Pierce County Sheriff's report, Nov. 9, 2006

MISSING PAINT CHIPS

Adding more incompetence to the investigation, the red paint chips found on Misty's jeans would turn up "missing." All that remained inside the bag where the chips were marked was a piece of plastic.

The lab technicians now had no way to match the red chips on Misty's jeans to Achziger's red Porsche.

Bober would claim that the red chips did match and the police were now trying to save face. Diana, however, no longer wants anything to do with him.

Bober would state that the police would tell Diana that they had, in fact, tested the red paint found on Misty's clothes against Achziger's Porsche. Bober discovered that the red paint was missing beforehand yet the police would lie to Diana about the test.

The lies and incompetence that began investigation have seemingly ended it as well. The Puyallup police relied far too heavily on polygraph tests to discount suspects where their own accounts (particularly in the case of Schmidt) were shaky at best. They failed to secure possession of Schmidt's Green Nova which may have proven to provide forensic evidence that Misty was in his vehicle.

Twenty-four years have elapsed since Misty's disappearance.

Her case remains unsolved.

THE CHOWCHILLA KIDNAPPINGS

KAREN HULSE

Chowchilla is a large farming community located about forty miles north of Fresno, California, in the dead center of the state. Named after the war-mongering nature of the area's American Indian settlers, the Yokuts, the name 'Chowchilla' translates to "murderers". Tributes to the Yokuts are still very present throughout Chowchilla, in art, school mascots, and tourist attractions.

Dwarfed next to other cities in the San Francisco Bay Area, Chowchilla drew little interest from anyone who was not a local or simply passing through to get to the coast. Chowchilla has no beautiful coastline to attract visitors or any notable industries like Silicon Valley. But it has instead maintained a small town feel through much of the 20th century as the surrounding area was booming with tech industry growth and skyrocketing housing prices.

Chowchilla's population has grown to over 18,000 and is home to several prisons and school districts. However, just forty years ago the town was home to less than 5,000 people. The small town community in 1970's Chowchilla made the events of July 15th, 1976, even more surprising than it otherwise would have been. After all, no one expected twenty-six grade schoolchildren to be kidnapped and buried alive in such a quiet farming neighborhood.

The Bus Ride Home

On the afternoon of July 15th, 1976, the Chowchilla summer school program was about to wrap up. During the summer months, the children were kept busy and out of the house with arts and crafts, swimming, and games in the park. Twenty-six children from the small farming town, ranging in age from 5 to 14 years old, came and went from the Dairyland Elementary School by school bus.

July 15th was to be the second-to-last scheduled day of the program for the summer, but the children had been having so much fun during the past few weeks that they crafted a petition to extend the program through the end of the month. The program was so popular that even the summer school teachers and the children's bus driver, Frank Edward "Ed" Ray, agreed to sign the petition for the children.

That morning was bright and sunny, so the children and their teachers had spent the day in the local community pool. Everyone swam and played with water balloons. On the bus ride home, many of the children were still wearing their damp bathing suits while others were wrapped up in beach towels. The bus ride home was filled with excitement over the potential for another couple weeks of summer school.

Everyone was happy and the adults had their guard down. School bus driver Ed was not overly suspicious when their path was blocked by a crippled van in the middle of the lane. They were driving down a narrow gravel road and he slowed as he came upon the van with its hood propped up. Since he was unable to easily pass the van, and due to the neighborly community that was Chowchilla at the time, Ed stopped the bus in order to offer help to the stranded travelers. Unfortunately for him and the children, this friendly gesture would be the beginning of a daylong nightmare for them all.

Kidnapped in Broad Daylight

As he brought the school bus to a stop, Ed opened the passenger doors to offer assistance to the drivers of the disabled van. But before he could even finish his offer, three men ambushed the bus with a rifle, handguns, and pantyhose pulled over their faces to obscure their appearance.

These three men were Fred Woods, Rick Schoenfeld, and Jim Schoenfeld. Rick and Jim were brothers and close friends with Fred, three desperate men looking to get rich without any consequence. Somewhere along their planning process, one of the men had crafted the harebrained scheme of kidnapping the community's young children and holding them hostage for ransom. Now here they were, ambushing a school bus full of young, terrified children who had just moments earlier been basking in the glow of a sunshiny day with their friends.

Fred, Rick, and Jim forced Ed into the back of the bus, as far away from the kidnappers as possible. With the one real threat to their plan trapped in the back of the bus, the three armed men took control of the wheel and began to drive the bus filled with children and the bus driver to an unknown location.

The children were terrified. Lynda Carrejo Labendeira, seated toward the front of the bus and just inches away from the men and their loaded guns, hid under her seat as the bus bumped across back roads and through bamboo thickets. Her three sisters were crying and panicked in the back of the bus while the rest of the schoolchildren sobbed, fearing for their lives.

They continued to drive through thick bamboo, tossing the bus from side-to-side with each stalk that the bus hit. The children continued to cower in fear as the school bus bumped and swayed through the thickets until eventually they arrived at a hidden ditch. Here, Ed and the children saw two vans parked in the small clearing, waiting for their arrival.

A Road Trip of Nightmares

The school bus stopped and the three men once again pointed their weapons at the children. Everyone, including Ed, were instructed to get into the back of the vans.

The windows of the vans were all painted black. The children could not see where they were and no one from the outside could see the abductees kept captive inside the vehicles.

It was a hot day, over one hundred degrees outside and the children had to relieve themselves.

Hours passed as the children grew hungry, sick, and the heat only amplified all of the sour smells filling the back of the vans. The children were dehydrated and ill, and no one knew what was going to happen when the vans eventually did stop.

For countless hours and miles, the vans continued to drive. Ed believed that the men were either taking them to a predetermined location or they were trying to stall for time. After what felt like an interminable drive, the vans finally came to a stop.

The kidnappers had arrived at their destination, a rock quarry in Livermore, California near San Francisco.

Buried Alive

The California Rock & Gravel Quarry was owner and operated by Fred Woods' father. The business was a busy one, but at night the grounds were entirely empty.

Under the dim illumination of construction lights, Fred, Rick, and Jim ordered everyone out of the now foul-smelling vans. The children and Ed pleaded with the men to explain what they were doing or where they were, but the only response they ever received was a rough, "Shut up and be quiet."

The children and Ed stumbled out of their cramped prisons into the quarry, and one-by-one their captors ordered each child to provide their name, age, address, and home phone number. After this information had been written down, the child was stripped of a single piece of clothing, to serve as proof of their hostages.

The armed men led their hostages through the empty quarry to a moving van buried under the quarry's surface. The van was hidden underground and nearly invisible from the surface, and the only way in or out of the cavity was by a long ladder.

It looked like one big coffin.

Once again pointing their weapons at the children, the three men ordered everyone down the ladder into the buried moving van. Each child carefully descended the ladder into the dusty, dark van, and once the last one had finished the journey, the men removed the ladder, blocked the door, and left.

An Underground Prison Cell

The buried moving van was stocked with only a few crude items, and not nearly enough to provide the hostages with any amount of comfort. There was old cereal, peanut butter, bread, and bottled water, but only enough of each to feed the children one pathetic meal. After going all day without food or water, these items did little to comfort the sickness overtaking most of the children.

There were several dirty mattresses scattered across the cell's floor, which frightened the children as they took them as a sign that they would be held in this underground prison for days or longer. A makeshift toilet was available in the form of a crude hole cut into the bottom of the moving van, but this offered little relief to the children.

The armed men had installed ventilation fans in the van's walls, in an attempt to keep the captives alive underground. However, several hours into the children's' captivity these fans failed and the prison cell began to fill with odors and fumes.

Many of the children were finally overcome by their sickness, and the smell of vomit, urine, and feces filled the airtight compartment. As hours passed, the children began to cry and scream, wishing for their parents to find them. With the little available food completely gone and conditions worsening, the hostages slowly began to accept that they might not ever leave this prison cell beneath the quarry.

The Last Hope

As the younger children succumbed to their exhaustion, sickness, and panic, Ed and the older children began to craft a last ditch plan to escape the underground holding cell. On the ceiling of the moving van was a removable metal panel, which offered the only chance the children and their bus driver had of escaping their prison. They began to drag the dirty mattresses across the van, piling them up underneath the panel. One by one, they drew closer to reaching the potential escape route.

Unfortunately, once they could reach the panel, they found that it was barricaded on top with a heavy truck battery and several feet of piled dirt. Together, Ed and the oldest of the boys pushed with all their strength, hoping to break free of the weight above them.

Finally, the panel shifted, and Ed and the boys were able to reach the dirt above them. The boys helped dig out the dirt piled above them, as the younger children watched or hid in case the captors returned. Many were afraid that they would be standing outside, watching for any attempt to escape from the underground prison. Despite the opportunity for escape, a palpable fear was in the air. If the men returned, the children were smart enough to realize they would be shot.

Exhausted and covered in dirt and filth, Ed and the boys finally broke free to the surface. They began lifting the younger children out of the moving van, with some standing on each other's shoulder in order to reach the escape panel. One by one, they emerged on the surface, and the hostages suddenly found themselves free after hours of torture, illness, and panic.

The group cautiously maneuvered the quarry, unsure of where their captors were hiding. Fortunately for Ed and the children, the three armed men were asleep during the entire escape. Thanks to a poorly timed nap, the kidnappers lost their hostages without any idea what was happening.

As they frantically searched for help, the group of children noticed a small building overlooking the quarry. One of the children, Lynda

Carrejo Labendeira, recalled that they found a man at one of the buildings.

"The gentleman came down and said, 'The world's been looking for you.'" With the entire community of Chowchilla searching for their missing children, news had spread far and wide in hopes of finding the children and their bus driver safe and sound.

With the help of this man, the authorities were alerted and medical help was sent to the quarry. The children were cleaned up and any dehydration or illness was treated. By July 17th, everyone had been returned home safely, where the families of the children welcomed them home with open arms.

The Hunt for the Kidnappers

At first, authorities had few leads to who might have kidnapped the children and their bus driver on July 15th. While Woods and the Schoenfeld brothers had attempted several times to call the local police with their ransom note, asking for $5 million for the safe return of the town's beloved children, so many frantic calls had been coming into the local dispatch station that they couldn't even get through to speak to authorities. Because they were never actually able to deliver their demands to the police, law enforcement were unsure of the motive when beginning their investigation.

With few leads, the police turned to an unusual tactic. Ed, the bus driver who had been held captive with the children, was put under hypnosis in an attempt to remember the license plate of one of the vans used to transport the group to the quarry and their underground prison. Miraculously, Ed did remember one of the plate numbers, which was traced back to the quarry owner's son, Fred Woods.

Fred Woods was arrested after running away from authorities and attempting to hide out in Vancouver, Canada. His partners, Rick and

Jim Schoenfeld, surrendered to authorities while still in California, after hearing that their accomplice had been arrested.

When investigating the trio, the police found a drafted ransom note, presumably what the men would have read to police if they had ever gotten through on the phone lines. They also found evidence that the men might have been inspired by High Pentecost's The Day the Children Vanished, which might have recently been checked out from the Chowchilla Public Library by one of the men.

All three men were from wealthy, privileged San Francisco Bay area families, and had no real reason to commit such a crime for money. Connections to child pornography, acts of violence, and other signs point to the fact that the three men were a twisted group of friends without a firm grip on their consciences. Jim Schoenfeld told commissioners that the ransom was dreamed up because he was in debt and jealous of the "Ferraris" and other luxuries that his neighbors owned. Woods stated that he didn't need the money, because he owned and operated a fruitful auto yard, but that his involvement in the crime was just motivated by greed. Either way, the men planned their kidnapping and ransom of the children for over a year before actually committing the crime.

Punishment for the Kidnappers

After their trial, each of the three kidnappers pleaded guilty to twenty-seven life sentences without the option of parole. Yet now, in 2017, only one of these men remains behind bars. Rick was released in 2012, and his brother Jim was given parole in 2015. Fred Woods currently remains in prison and is ineligible for parole until 2018. Ever since the first Schoenfeld brother was released from prison, tension has risen among the Chowchilla community. But there are none as concerned as the now-adult victims of these men.

"We felt safe in Chowchilla," said Lynda Carrejo Labendeira, now a grown woman with a family of her own. She was referring to the fact that, for many years, everyone in Chowchilla felt safe knowing that the terrible men that had kidnapped twenty-six of their community's young children would be stuck behind bars forever. The kidnappers' lifetime imprisonment was a comfort to their victims, who were terrified of what the men might be capable of if released from their sentences.

Unfortunately, all three of the men were granted eligibility for parole when an appeals court reviewed their sentences. The reasoning for this decision was that Woods and the Schoenfeld brothers did no physical bodily harm to the children or bus driver that they held hostage for over eighteen hours.

The Schoenfeld brothers have both been freed from prison at this time. Many of the victims and their families feel that the victims' emotional wellbeing has been completely overlooked in the decision to release these criminals.

Woods' Parole Trial

The Schoenfeld brothers' attorney advocates for the eventual release of Woods, claiming that he is no danger to his past victims. However, with a past of rule breaking, child pornography, and illicit cell phone use, Woods' chances of being paroled in the near future are slim-to-none. With the other two kidnappers out free on the streets, this is little comfort to the community of Chowchilla.

In 2015, Woods was eligible to apply for parole. Unlike his accomplices, though, this venture was not successful. Citing Woods' many "disciplinary infractions" while in prison, as well as three instances of possession of pornography, some of it featuring minors, and two instances of possessing a contraband phone, Jill Klinge, an attorney in Alameda County, did not believe that Woods deserved parole.

David Linn, the District Attorney for Madera County, where Chowchilla is located, mentioned that because of Woods' "privileged background" the convict was unwilling to follow the rules – of life or of prison. Linn also credited some of the kidnapping victims who had come forward at the trial for Wood's denial of parole, stating that they had given statements that "tugged at the heartstrings."

Despite the overwhelming disdain for Woods, his parole drew many noteworthy supporters. Palo Alto Representative Anna Eshoo wrote to the court stating that Woods had "paid his debt to society." Even some of the kidnapping victims said that they believed Woods had served his time and deserved to rejoin society.

Lasting Effects

Life after the kidnapping has been very rough for many of the children. Symptoms of P.T.S.D. are rampant throughout the twenty-six children. Many of them report experiencing panic attacks and nightmares for years after the kidnapping actually occurred. One even shot a tourist with BB gun when the man parked his car outside of the survivor's home. Decades after the kidnapping, several of the children suffer from substance abuse problems or have spent time in prison for behavioral issues, much of which has been linked to the trauma experienced in their childhood.

After committing the largest kidnapping in United States history, there was little mercy available to Woods and the Schoenfeld brothers. After decades in prison, they are now being presented with a lawsuit pursued by many of their victims from the kidnapping in 1976. This lawsuit is meant to reflect the immense emotional trauma that the children underwent during their kidnapping at gunpoint and subsequent imprisonment.

Jennifer Hyde, who is now almost fifty years old, told the media that she is still afraid of the dark decades after the kidnapping occurred. In fact, until very recently, she could only sleep when there was a nightlight on in her bedroom. She also reported having nightmares where she died and was attending or one funeral, which she connected to the belief that she was going to die that day in the buried moving truck.

Hyde also claims that her family suffers from her experience as a child. "[My] children don't get to lead a normal life," she said, which she blames on the fact she is overprotective and terrified of something similar happening to her own children as what happened to her in 1976. When her first child started kindergarten, Hyde skipped work everyday to follow her son's school bus and ensure that he arrived safely at a friend's house.

Remembering a Hero

Edward "Ed" Ray, the children's bus driver and the man largely responsible for their escape, was awarded a citation for outstanding community service, and February 26th is officially Edward Ray Day in Chowchilla, California. Many of the children he helped rescue that day continued to keep in touch and visit him until his death on May 17th, 2012.

Without the help of Ed that day, who knows what would have happened to the children. While the events of July 15th, 1976, might be near-forgotten in the minds of many Chowchilla residents, it would be a travesty to let the heroic actions of Ed Ray become nothing more than a story told in the history books. When faced with a dangerous threat, whether it is a man with a gun or a wild animal, it truly says something about a man whether he protects himself first or acts in order to protect those who depend on him. On July 15ht, 1976, Edward "Ed" Ray was the latter.

The Chowchilla Kidnappings in Pop Culture

While the kidnapping may have been inspired by a short story itself, many replications of the events have appeared in television and movies. An episode of Walker, Texas Ranger, starring Chuck Norris, involved a school bus kidnapping that closely matched the real-life events in Chowchilla. A made-for-television, full-length film called They've Taken Our Children was a popular telling of the Chowchilla kidnappings. The events of July 15th, 1976, have also been covered on countless true crime television programs throughout the years.

The Chinchilla kidnapping, while certainly not the most famous true crime in history, has become one of many tropes when it comes to almost-too-ridiculous-to-be-true scenarios found on primetime television shows. While the Chinchilla kidnappings may not be referenced directly, situations where crowds of people, whether students on a school bus or commuters on a train are kidnapped as a group are commonly seen on shows like CSI, Without a Trace, and NCIS.

Chowchilla Today

Now, many of Chowchilla's citizens think little of the kidnapping that occurred over 40 years ago. Because of Chowchilla's quick growth, the majority of its current residents either moved to Chowchilla after 1976, or were not born or old enough to remember the hysteria that erupted around the traumatic incident. Most people who were alive during the kidnapping only think of that day when news reports mention anniversaries or trials for the kidnappers. But for the victims, who are now almost all adults with children of their own, the events of their childhood come to mind every single day.

Many of the children who were kidnapped that day, including Jennifer Hyde, have moved out of Chowchilla or California. Some are running away from the memories of their childhood, while others have moved for less sinister reasons like career opportunities or family. Sadly for Hyde, her brother, Jeff Hyde, who was also kidnapped from the school bus that day, was killed in an accident at the age of fifteen. With a childhood filled with tragic events, it is no wonder that Jennifer Hyde left her hometown.

It is understandable why the city of Chowchilla doesn't want to dwell on the events of over forty years ago, and instead wants to move on and paint a new image of itself for the nation. The kidnapping has now become part of history. Everyone made it back home to his or her family, and that is that. However, this doesn't erase the events of July 15th, 1976, from the past, and, while the only sources that bring up the kidnapping at this point are true crime enthusiasts and media reporters, the kidnapping of twenty-six schoolchildren from a bus remains a vivid part of the town's history.

BONUS:

It was a warm summer morning on January 26, 1966, when the three Beaumont children left their suburban home to celebrate Australia Day at the beach. The children regularly made the trip by themselves, so their mother felt at ease providing them with bus fare and sending them on their way while she visited and had lunch with a close friend. However, she would return home that afternoon to find that the children still had not returned. That morning would end up being the last time she saw her three children.

Jane (aged 9), Arnna (aged 7), and Grant (aged 4), lived in Somerton Park, a quiet suburb minutes away from Adelaide, South Australia. Their father, Jim Beaumont, was a linen goods salesman who frequently traveled for work and their mother, Nancy Beaumont, was a stay-at-home mother.

The oldest child, Jane, was viewed by her parents as responsible enough to supervise the other children for short trips and adventures, a style of parenting that was the norm in Australia at that time. The children frequently took the five-minute bus ride to neighboring Glenely Beach by themselves and were looking forward to celebrating the national holiday at the beach.

The children left their home at 10:00am that morning and were seen arriving at the beach by witnesses at 10:15am. They spent much of that morning at play on the beach and were supposed to arrive home at 2:00pm. When they did not arrive at the appointed time, their mother assumed that they had become preoccupied with celebrating the holiday with their playmates and that they would arrive on the next bus or had decided to walk home, something that the three children had done before. When the children did not disembark from the next scheduled bus, their mother began to grow worried.

The disappearance of the Beaumont children would result in one of the largest manhunts and police investigations in Australian history. Furthermore, the event had widespread consequences on Australian society, shattering the illusion that many parents had regarding their children's safety and changing the way that Australians parented their children forever.

Timeline of Events

10:00am - The children leave their Somerton Park home to travel to Glenely Beach by bus.

10:15am - They are seen exiting the bus by multiple witnesses.

11:00am - The three children are spotted playing beneath a sprinkler by an elderly woman. A tall blond man is spotted lying on the ground next to them, watching the children play.

11:15am - A tall blond man is seen playing with the children. They all appear to be laughing and at ease.

11:45am - The children purchase several pastries and a meat pie from the beach snack shop.

12:15pm - The tall blond man and the children are seen leaving the beach together. The children are witnessed laughing together and holding hands.

3:00pm - A postman on his route spots the children walking along Jetty Road alone, away from the beach. The postman is known to the children and they exchange greetings. Police believe that the timeline for this event is incorrect.

7:20pm - The parents of the children become gravely concerned and file a missing children's report with the local police department. Jim Beaumont and the local police search the entire Glenely Beach area.

8:40pm - Police search the surrounding beaches with no results. The father contacts friends and relatives in an attempt to locate the children.

10:00pm - Police issue public radio announcements with a missing children report.

Points of Interest

There are several details in this story which raised doubts with both the parents of the children and the local police department. When the children departed for Glenely Beach in the morning of January 26th, they left with only enough money to cover their bus fare: six shilling and a sixpence. However, the shop owner, who sold several pastries and a meat pie to the children at 11:45am, reported that the children paid for the food with a $1 bill, an amount of money that they did not have when they left their mother's care.

In addition, the shop owner knew the children well and had sold them food and pastries several times before. He reported that the children had never purchased a meat pie before. This suggests that the children received the money from someone after leaving their parents home and that they may have been purchasing the meat pie for someone else.

Lastly, the mother of the children, Nancy Beaumont, repeatedly said that her children were quite shy and very unlikely to speak with strangers, indicating that they may have met the tall blond man prior to the date of their disappearance. Their mother also remembered a seemingly innocuous comment from Arnna, who had previously told her mother that Jane had "got a boyfriend down the beach." Nancy assumed that her daughter was referring to a young playmate, but in hindsight it seems that she may have been referring to the tall blond man spotted by witnesses.

Police Investigation

The South Australian police force began investigating the disappearance of the children in full-force the evening of their disappearance. After interviewing several witnesses who were present at Glenely Beach, they were able to determine that the children were playing with a tall blond, "thin-faced" man while at the beach. He was described as being a blond man in his late 30s with a thin or athletic build.

"Things seemed bungled from the get-go," forensic psychologist Paula Orange said. "First off, the artist drawing the picture admitted to being drunk at the time of completing his task. So the sketch made of the suspect looks more like a lantern-jawed alien than a real person. Secondly, the witnesses claimed that the man was in his late thirties. Witnesses are notorious for getting ages wrong and the police dismissed too many possible subjects out of hand because they didn't fit the profile."

Several witnesses stated that the man was seen dressing the children prior to leaving the beach. The children's parents said that the kids, especially Jane, were very shy and unlikely to speak to a stranger. This later led police to theorize that the children had met the man in question prior to the date of their disappearance and had grown to know him over a period of several weeks.

The blond man and three children were seen leaving the beach together at 12:15pm, after the children purchased several pastries and a meat pie from a local vendor with a $1 bill, an amount of money that they did not have when they left their home that morning.

A wrench was thrown into the investigation when a postman, who knew the children and was on friendly terms with them, reported that he saw the children around 3:00pm that afternoon walking away from the beach and in the direction of their home in Somerton Park. He stated that he exchanged greetings with the young children and that they seemed to be in good spirits. In particular, the postman said that he say the children were "holding hands and laughing" as they walked down the road alone, with no blond companion in sight. Police later said that they believed the postman was mistaken about the timeline and that he most likely saw the children walking some time before noon.

Several months later, a woman in a nearby neighborhood contacted police and told them that she had seen a man with two girls and a young boy enter an abandoned house on her street. She also reported seeing the young boy walking away from the house before he was roughly grabbed by, and returned to the house with, the older man. She never saw the man or children again.

"The response from the public was overwhelming," Orange said. "People drove from miles away to aid in the search. They combed the beach and drained part of it all to no avail. They found nothing, not a trace."

The police were quickly able to eliminate drowning as the cause of the children's disappearance as a result of several witnesses saying that they saw the children leave the beach around 12:15pm. Furthermore, all of the children's belongings were missing, lending further support to the theory that they left the beach. After speaking with the parents, the police were able to identify seventeen different items that were carried by the children that day, providing a list of items that could be used to identify their remains or whereabouts. However, the police's continue efforts continued to prove fruitless.

The Psychic Circus

On November 8, 1966, nearly a year after the children's initial disappearance, an internationally-renowned psychic from the Netherlands, Gerard Croiset, was flown to Australia to investigate the case. His presence caused a whirlwind of media coverage in Australia and across the world. After making a series of outlandish and ever-changing claims, Croiset claimed that the children were buried underneath a warehouse just minutes away from the children's school.

"I appreciate him (Gerard Croiset) coming out to find the children," Jim Beaumont said. "But I don't believe what he said. I don't believe the children are dead and will continue to believe until given evidence that proves otherwise."

The building, which was under construction at the time of their disappearance, was eventually razed and excavated after the owners raised $40,000 for the project as a result of public pressure. No evidence of the children or their belongings were ever found.

"The press and police followed Croiset around everywhere," Orange said. "He was an obvious con artist but they were desperate. They had nothing."

A Series of Letters

Beginning in 1968, the parents of the three children began to receive a series of letters which rekindled hope in the idea that their children may still be alive. Postmarked from Dandernong, Victoria, the series of letters claimed to be written by Jane, the eldest daughter. She claimed to be under the supervision of a man and in good health and care, saying

Dear Mum and Dad,

We had a beautiful lunch today...The man is feeding us really well. The man took us to see The Sound of Music yesterday.

Police officers believed the letters to be from Jane after comparing them to examples of her handwriting and, as far as 1981, the Sidney Morning Herald produced analysis from handwriting experts claiming that the letters were actually from the missing child.

Following receipt of the letters supposedly sent from Jane, the parents received a letter from a man claiming to be in possession of the children. He said that he was willing to hand the children over to the parents at a specific time and location. The Beaumonts arrived at the appointed time and location with an undercover police officer but no one showed. They later received a letter from the same man claiming that he saw the undercover police officer arrive with the parents and that he would now keep the children, ending any hope of a peaceful exchange.

In 1992, following another investigation and remarkable achievements in fingerprint technology, authorities identified the author of the letters as a local man who was just a teenager at the time of the hoax. He reportedly wrote and mailed the letters as "a joke."

False Closure

Then, in November 2013, South Australian police received an anonymous tip claiming that the children were buried underneath a warehouse located in North Plympton. Although radar identified "one small anomaly, which can indicate movement or objects within the soil," no evidence was ever found.

The Suspects

Bevan Spencer von Einem

Bevan Spencer von Einem has long been considered the prime suspect in the disappearance of the Beaumont children. Einem was convicted of the July 1983 murder of fifteen-year-old Richard Kelvin, son of a popular news reporter, in 1984. Police have long suspected Einem of working with a series of accomplices and of having committed other abductions and murders.

In 1983, a police informant known as "Mr. B" told police that Einem claimed to have taken three children from a beach to perform medical "experiments," claiming that he performed "brilliant surgery" on the three children before accidentally killing one of them. Following the child's accidental death, the informant stated that Einem claimed to have killed the other two children and buried them in an open field outside the city of Adelaide.

Einem did bare some resemblance to the descriptions of the tall blond man given to police following the disappearance of the Beaumont children and was known to frequent Glenely Beach to spy on people in the changing rooms. He was also noted as having an obsession with children.

Einem worked as an accountant and lived with his mother. There were rumors that he was part of a ring of Adelaide professionals who shared a "hobby" of kidnapping, drugging and raping boys.

"Einem did match the description of the police sketches," Orange said. "And he did like to frequent the same beach. He seemed more interested in young teenage males as his list of known victims would indicate. Einem was a homosexual who picked up hitchhikers with his transvestite friend where they would engage in a "rough trade" style of sex. He would take photographs of his victims as a keepsake. The three young children would seem to be outside of his modus operandi."

However, Einem was significantly younger than the suspect described by witnesses; Einem was around 20 years old at the time, while the description of the suspect placed him in his late 20s. But, in 2007 local police officers identified a young man who looked exactly like a young Einem in Channel 7 news footage of the incident taken days after the disappearance. He remains a prime suspect in the case.

"The newly found news footage does implicate Einem in a psychological way," Orange said. "Killers often like to return to the scene of the crime. He was spotted on film, days after the disappearance. What are the odds against that?"

Arthur Stanley Brown

Arthur Stanley Brown, along with Einem, is considered to be one of two prime suspects in the abduction of the Beaumont children. In

1988, Brown, then 86 years old, was charged with kidnapping, raping, and murdering Judith and Susan Mackey in Townsville, Queensland. His first trial was declared a mistrial after the jury failed to reach a verdict in the case and his second trial was blocked because he was declared unfit to stand trial; Brown was suffering from dementia and Alzheimer's disease by this time.

He is considered one of two prime suspects in the case because of his connection to the murder of other children and because of his remarkable resemblance to descriptions of the tall blond man seen with the children at the time of their disappearance. He was also a prime suspect in the Adelaide Oval case, which involved the disappearance of Joanna Ratcliffe and Kirste Gordon.

"Brown was a known pedophile by his closest family members," Orange said. "He is alleged to have molested numerous younger relatives. He could be placed in the same area and time of the Beaumont children but nothing could be proven."

Although Brown is considered to be a prime suspect in the disappearance of the Beaumont children, the suspect in the case was identified as being in his late 30s; Brown was in his 50s at the time. Brown died in 2002 without ever admitting to the crime.

"Brown would move into a nursing home at the end of his life," Orange said. "He would die an innocent man with the courts never able to officially charge him because of his Alzheimer's."

James Ryan O'Neill

James Ryan O'Neill, convicted of murdering nine-year-old Ricky John Smith in the Australian state of Tasmania in 1975 and currently serving a life sentence for the crime, was considered as a suspect in the Beaumont children disappearance for some time. He is reported as having told several friends in the early 1970s that he was responsible for the disappearance of the Beaumont children in 1966. However, he was publicly eliminated as a suspect by the South Australian police. He remains in prison in Tasmania to this day.

"O'Neill was the subject of a documentary called 'The Fishermen'," Orange said. "In the documentary, he is evasive about being the man behind the disappearance of the children. He is, however, at the forefront of most pundits who have studied the story. While Brown and Einem did not have charming personas, O'Neill did. He was handsome and smiley with the ability to manipulate everyone around him. He could fabricate lies at the drop of a hat so it is easy to believe that he would be able to charm the children into his acquaintance. People who knew him all described him as 'the most likable man you'll ever meet.' No one could believe that he would be capable of such an act."

Derek Ernest Percy

In 2007, the Victorian newspaper The Age published a report stating that Derek Ernest Percy, at the time the longest-serving prisoner in the southeastern Australian state, was responsible for the disappearance of the Beaumont children in 1966. Initially jailed in 1970 for the 1969 murder of 12-year-old Yvonne Tuohy, Percy was found not guilty of the crime by reason of insanity, but was nonetheless jailed "indefinitely."

He is widely considered to be Australia's worst child serial killer and is suspected of the killings of the Beaumont children, as well as the abduction, attempted rape, and stabbing of Marianne Schmidt and Christine Sharrock on January 11, 1965. In October 2014, Percy was also ruled to have abducted and killed seven-year-old Linda Stilwell in

1968. However, Percy passed away from cancer in 2013, having never admitted to any of his crimes. He remains a possible suspect in the case.

"Percy is unique in that he may have had his mother not aiding him but covering up for him," Orange said. "He is certainly one of the most sadistic pedophiles on record, his doings are unmentionable out of respect for his victims. He was in the city at the time of the Beaumont children disappearance and is probably the top suspect along with O'Neill. His mother, however, has thrown out a lot of what could have been evidence in the case."

Related Cases

Two similar cases to the disappearance of the Beaumont children attracted widespread attention in the South Australian media, and the primary suspect in the Beaumont children's kidnapping case was convicted in one case and suspected in the other.

The Adelaide Oval Case

On August 25, 1972, two young girls, Joanne Ratcliffe (aged 11) and Kirste Gordon (aged 4) went missing while attending an Australian football game. They are presumed dead. This case also received widespread attention in the South Australian media and Bevan Spencer von Einem was considered the primary suspect in their disappearance.

Einem matched the descriptions of the tall blond man provided by witnesses in the Beaumont children's case and closely resembles the police sketch released to the public. A private police report in leaked in 1989 identified Einem as the primary suspect in the case.

The Family Murders

From 1973 to 1983, a group of men is believed to have been involved in the abduction, rape, and murder of a series of young men and male teenagers in the Adelaide area. Five teens were killed during this time period, including Alan Barnes (aged 16), Neil Muir (aged 25), Peter Stogneff (aged 14), Mark Langley (aged 18), and Richard Kelvin (aged 15). All victims were abducted and subjected to extended bouts of torture and physical assault, including sexual assault and medical experimentation.

Bevan Spencer von Einem was convicted of the abduction and murder of Richard Kelvin 1984 and is currently serving life in prison in Port Augusta prison. In 1990, he was also charged with the murder of Alan Barnes and Mark Langley, but key evidence from the Richard Kelvin murder was ruled inadmissible in the trial. Following the ruling against this key evidence, the prosecution dropped these charges against Einem on December 21, 1990.

Although Einem was the only member of this group to be convicted, and four out of five of The Family Murders remain unsolved, law enforcement officials believe that Einem was part of a white-collar group that preyed on young children. He remains the prime, and only living, suspect in the disappearance of the Beaumont children.

Impact on the Parents

Jim and Nancy Beaumont continued to hold out hope of finding their children for several decades after their disappearance. In fact, the couple continued to live at the Somerton Park home, at 109 Harding Street, that they shared with their children for nearly two decades, hoping that the children would return home someday. Nancy Beaumont was reported as saying that it would be "dreadful" if the children returned to the home only to find that their parents had moved.

"The Beaumonts left the rooms of the children untouched," Orange said. "Every toy, every book even the bed was left exactly as the children had left them."

The couple were never considered as suspects in the case and cooperated with the police at every turn in the investigation, including working with the police and searching in vain every time a new lead developed in the case over the next several decades.

According to The Age, the parents "have since separated, but still live in Adelaide." The stress and sorrow that resulted from their children's abduction, combined with the constant new leads and media attention is said to have contributed to the failure of their marriage.

Jim, in particular, is said to still be suffering from intense and inconsolable grief every time a new development is reported. Nancy was also reported to have suffered extreme grief and horror when, in 1990, several Australian newspapers released computer-generated images of what her children would look like after aging several decades. She reportedly refused to look at the pictures.

"Jim was a little bit stronger than Nancy," Orange said. "He would address the media more than she did. But they both suffered terribly for the rest of their lives into their eighties. They would spend over fifty years wishing for their children's return, getting false hope after false hope, one false lead after another which would all ultimately turn up nothing. It was a horrific cruelty."

Lastly, Jim and Nancy have largely been seen as sympathetic and pitiable figures in the Australian media and in society at large. Although their actions may seem reckless or irresponsible by today's standards, Australian society was viewed as extremely safe in the 1960s and their policy of allowing a child to supervise their younger siblings both in the home and in public was practiced by a large portion of Australian parents.

Impact on Australian Society

The disappearance of the Beaumont children became an overnight sensation in Australia, led to one of the largest police searches in the country's history, and remains the most famous missing persons case in the country. Prior to this incident, Australia was largely viewed as one of the safest societies on the planet and children were allowed to roam freely, doors remained unlocked at all times, and there was little fear of strangers. All of that changed overnight.

"Australia lost its innocence with the disappearance of the Beaumont Children," Orange said. "For three young children to disappear was unheard of. The city where they grew up was a dignified place, a safe place. But it was all an illusion that went away the day the children went missing."

During the initial search for the children, Jim Beaumont went on national television to appeal for their safe return. His heartfelt address to the nation had a lasting impact on the parents and children who watched his plea. Hundreds of viewers called into the station to offer tips and Australian police report that hundreds of tips continue to come in every year to this day. His image on national television continues to serve as a warning for those who believe in the incorruptibility of their fellow citizens and in the safety of their country.

"A lot of people today will blame the parents for letting them go on the bus alone," Adelaide resident Rachel Harding said. "But times were different back then. Back then kids would walk to school by themselves. Kids were told not to talk to strangers. The Beaumonts did tell their children to not talk to children. But child molesters are cunning monsters. My guess is that he may have stolen the eldest child's purse then conned them into seeing him as their benefactor. They would not have had money to get home then along comes this "blonde man" who offers them money. Buys them food and promises to take them home."

Children who came of age in Australia during the 1960s have remarked that there was a definite culture shift following the Beaumont children's disappearance, often describing a "before" and "after." While children were once allowed to roam freely and interact with strangers, Australian parents have since altered their style of parenting and curtailed the amount of freedom offered to young children.

"It was the type of case where we believe there was a lone offender," Australian police detective Des Bray said. "It isn't the type of crime where one would go around bragging about. But we do hope that he told someone and that somebody knows something."

If the Beaumont children are alive today, they would all be in their 50s and would have lived through years of hearing their names and story broadcast on national television and reported on breathlessly in national newspapers. Despite the vast amount of information we have on the case, their fates may never be known with any certainty.

Both Jim and Nancy Beaumont are still alive, and as of this writing they are ninety and eighty-years old respectively. The anonymous tips and false hopes continue to come in today as they did over fifty years ago.

THE KIDNAPPING OF EDGARDO MORTARA

DARA ROSEN

It is easy to look at the past with a modern eye and criticize the actions of our ancestors by comparing them to the socio-political scene today. And while it is practically impossible to avoid doing that, we should scrutinize cases such as the kidnapping of Edgardo Mortara with as much knowledge of our own biases and worldviews as we can. The political context that Edgardo grew up in is very dissimilar to the one in modern Italy. Italy as a unified country hadn't truly existed yet, and the Pope, who at that time was Pope Pius IX, ruled over a swath of territory far larger than Vatican City is today. Christian laws, beyond what people commonly refer to as the Ten Commandments, were in full force at this time, and some of them will be at least a little confusing to our modern readership.

Edgardo Levi Mortara was born to upper class Jewish parents. Unbeknownst to them, and without Edgardo's consent, his maidservant baptized him when he was an infant. There were four distinct, if obscure, laws that governed those actions, and it should be said that Edgardo's case was not unique, even though these sorts of happenings were rare. The four laws were these: Jewish children could not be abducted from Jewish parents, Jewish children could not be baptized without parental consent, non-Christian parents could not raise Christian children, and baptism automatically created a Christian child. However, if a Jewish child was thought to be dying, they could be baptized in order to save their souls, and parental consent was no longer necessary. Edgardo, in his infancy, had caught a terrible sickness, at least in the maid's perspective, and according to her testimony she did what she felt she must to save him. Through the contested power of this backroom baptism, Edgardo became a Christian boy and Christians were not allowed to be raised by non-Christians. The Church was forced by their own rules to step in.

Even in these first few details, there are controversies. Did the maidservant, known as Anna "Nina" Morisi, actually know how to perform a proper baptismal service, and if not, was it still valid? Did she fabricate that part of the story? Was Edgardo as sick as he seemed? The conflicting pieces of evidence trying to answer those questions and more surround the Mortara case. Some of them have remained mysteries for more than the hundred and fifty years that have since passed. Can this case still be known as a kidnapping when we take the events that followed his governmental seizure into consideration? In any circumstance, Edgardo's case quickly diverged into two competing versions that spread internationally and threatened the existing political power structures that existed in Italy at the time. As time went on, it is likely that both versions of the story gained merit in their own right. However, in the midst of the opposing sides composed of Jewish newspapers, Catholic newspapers, and multiple governments friendly to either the Papal States section of Italy, or the government in charge of Italian Unification, was a Jewish family and their missing son.

Edgardo, The Boy

Edgardo was the third youngest of eight siblings. His mother and father were Marianna and Salomone "Momolo" Mortara, and his birth date was August 27th, 1851, which was shortly after the family moved from the Duchy of Modena to Bologna, which was one of the Papal Legations in the far north of the Pope-controlled region. Just shortly after Edgardo was born, Anna Morisi came onto the scene as the family's new servant; she was 18 years old and illiterate at the time. At the time, Catholics were technically forbidden from working in non-Christian households, but there were far fewer Jewish families in the area than there were Christians. Approximately 200 Jewish families lived in Bologna by 1858, and many of them were merchants. Slightly less than 300 years ago, all of the Jewish people in the area had been expelled. The religious tensions had been swept underground since then. Despite the rule, many of the Jewish families in Bologna could afford servants and many of them took on Catholic servants as a result of the local demographics available to them. On top of that, Catholic maids could still work during Jewish Sabbath days, which made them invaluable to busy families.

Sometime between then and when Morisi because pregnant in 1855, Edgardo had gotten sickly enough that Morisi felt compelled to do something about it. The family doctor later confirmed that Edgardo was about age one at the time of the instigating sickness. Edgardo had previously lost a sibling to an illness, and at that time another Catholic maid had confided in Morisi that the Mortara's servant should have baptized the boy. Morisi allegedly responded that she hadn't baptized him, but that she had learned how to do it since that unfortunate tragedy and had performed the rite on Edgardo. Once Morisi began to show her pregnancy, the Mortara family paid for her to stay at a midwife's home to carry her child to term in a quiet, easy environment. Common practice back then was just to fire a pregnant maidservant, which was a somewhat common occurrence with unmarried servants. However, on top of providing Morisi with a safe, healthy pregnancy, the Mortara's lied on her behalf and told their neighbours that she had taken ill and returned to her home in the San Giovanni village in Persiceto. Once her newborn had been taken to an adoption centre, as was required by the Papal States of unwed mothers, Morisi returned to the Mortara's to serve as their servant for another year. After that, she took up work with another Jewish family in the area, and then in less than a year she had married and moved out of Bologna. Despite all of the kindnesses shown to her by the Mortaras, Morisi was still living in a time where women were treated terribly for almost all the decisions they were allowed to make, and when the time came, she quickly submitted what she had done with Edgardo to an inquisitor. Likely, she was afraid of what would happen to her if she was caught lying for the Mortara's benefits, but her real reasoning for not protecting her previous employer is unknown.

Edgardo was a healthy six year old when he was taken from his family, and many said he was the shine in his mother's eyes. It was regrettable and suspicious that the inquisitors waited some five years after the backroom baptism to finally act and investigate the baptism rumours. Throughout those five years, Edgardo had been raised as a Jewish boy, and it is hard to imagine how anyone could think that he was a Christian child. The religious and military police serving the Pope, known as the carabinieri, came to the Mortara residence slightly after the sun had set on June 23rd, 1858. After having some conversation with them, the leader of the carabinieri, Marshal Pietro Lucidi, told them: "Signor Mortara, I am sorry to inform you that you are the victim of a betrayal". Although Lucidi, if not others, was sympathetic to the Mortara's plight, he had to follow the orders of the Bologna inquisitor, a Dominican friar named Father Pier Gaetano Feletti. After witnessing the agony that his visit and declaration wrought about the Mortara family, Feletti granted them a final night with their son. He was quoted as saying: "[I] would have a thousand times preferred to be exposed to much more serious dangers in performing my duties than to have to witness such a painful scene." The family fought the removal of their son the best they could: they drafted an appeal for Bologna's cardinal legate and the archbishop, but neither of these people were in the city at the time. After pleading with Feletti, the man denied him, stated that Edgardo would be well taken care of under the Pope's protection, and that Momolo Mortara should not make a fuss when the carabinieri returned or there would be bigger problems.

That evening, Edgardo was whisked away amidst familial tears and tears of the policeman who had been standing guard. At first, the

Mortaras had no way of knowing where their son had been taken, but eventually found out that he had been placed in the House of Catechumens. There, it was said that Edgardo quickly became fascinated by Christian and by some accounts developed into a prodigy. He was able to recite full verses and sermons. The story diverges about whether or not this is true, but either Edgardo was happily working as a Christian at such a young age, or coerced and deeply missing his family, remains to be seen. However, the older Edgardo became, the more he willingly took part in the Church and grew close with the Pope. He said in his later years that around the age of 13, he often wrote to his parents "dealing with religion and doing what I could to convince them of the truth of the Catholic faith." His faith was nonetheless a sticking point for Jewish communities in the Papal States and abroad. As time passed, the entire Jewish diaspora wanted to see him returned to his family, while the Catholic church used his story to prove their own religious narrative.

The Mortaras Versus the Pope

The Mortara family appealed several times. They questioned the inquisitor Feletti's decision and Morisi's story as soon as they tracked down who had reported a secret baptism. They rallied support from the Jewish diaspora as well as from their local community. They wanted their son back, and they would do anything within their power to see him returned. Marianna Mortara was portrayed as the broken mother, and was sometimes encouraged to act it up or to act in certain ways so that her position would not be questioned. The extended family began gathering as much information as they could in order to prove their case. However, most of their work would fall upon deaf ears. The capital was under no obligation to listen to them, at least at first, and so it simply ignored their plight.

One of their first steps in the appeal process was to locate Morisi. Marianna's younger brother, Angelo Padovani, tricked a relation of Morisi's into telling them that she had heard that Morisi had been the one talk to Feletti. Together with Marianna's brother-in-law, Cesare De Angelis, Padovani tracked down Morisi. Justifiably scared of them and of the results of her own actions, Morisi tearfully recounted what she had told to Feletti during an interrogation. She claimed that she had not wanted to see Edgardo separated from his family, and was deeply disturbed that that had happened. Momolo was convinced by the emotions in her story that she was telling them the truth, and left her residence to find a witness and a notary, but when the group of them returned a couple of hours later, Morisi was long gone. The Mortaras would not see her again. Their next steps for reconciliation were to take her verbal story and information they gathered about Morisi from their neighbours and her colleagues to the authorities. There were stories spreading of Morisi's sexual impropriety, which the press backing Mortara quickly used to discredit her version of the events. An additional damning factor was that Morisi had claimed a local grocer had taught her how to perform the baptism, but the grocer claimed to have no recollection of her and that he had no idea how to go about such a sacrosanct ritual.

Momolo travelled to Rome on several occasions to try and win back his son. Once, Marianna accompanied him in the hopes that her presence would convince Edgardo to sneak back with them. Hearing that they were coming, one of the rectors in charge of Edgardo's care spirited him to Altari, a town nearly 100km away. Undeterred, the family presses onward to Altari, however, the mayor of the town has them arrested upon arrival. At that point, they are forced back to Rome. However, the amount of negative press that the Church was already attracting over the Mortara issue forces the Cardinal Secretary of State Giacomo Antonelli, also known as the Pope's right-hand-man, to force the rector to return Edgardo to the capital. It was in this way that mother and son were finally reunited, despite the reunion being short lived.

When his parents visited him at the Catechumens, there arose two very different stories. The story that the Mortaras told was that Edgardo was somewhat sickly, desperately wanted to be with his Jewish family, and wanted to remain Jewish. Marianna said that "he had lost weight and turned pale; his eyes were filled with terror ... I told him that he was born a Jew like us and like us he must always remain one and he replied: 'Si, mia cara mamma, I will never forget to say the Sherma every day.'" The priests present at these meetings also badgered the Mortara family to become Christians so that they could have their son left. Reportedly, the Mortara's left very frightened. The story told by the Pope and his associates was that Edgardo truly wanted to be a Christian and that he wanted his parents to be Christians. Pro-Catholic newspapers announced that Edgardo's mother had ripped off the Virgin Mary broach from his neck and in other reports claimed that she had screamed: "I'd rather see you dead than a Christian!"

Politics and Religion in 19th Century Italy

The separation of Church and State is something that many people take for granted today, but at the time Edgardo was alive, the two powers were one. Thus, much of the discussion of the Mortara case revolves around religion as much as it does around politics. One of the most persuasive arguments put forth by the Church's critics was that by taking Edgardo away from his parents, they were violating his ability to follow out the Ten Commandments. The Pro-Church side of the argument became anti-Semitic in its worse iterations. It is crucial to note that there was underlying and often overt Antisemitism in these areas for hundreds of years, which might explain Edgardo's reluctance to return and his easy conversion to Christianity. As much as his parents wanted him back, it was safer for a young Semitic boy to be Christian in that area of the world.

Another point to note is that the Pope might not have been involved with the Mortara case from the beginning, but the response by the international presses had certainly irritated him. There was an ongoing debate about whether or not the Pope was the one making the decisions about the Mortara case; however, once he was backed into a corner by the constant criticism, the Pope acted as any person would. He got defensive and, without looking into the matter further, declared that it would be against Church policy to send the Christian boy back to his non-Christian parents. He stood firm on this issue for the rest of his term as Pope. On a yearly basis, the Pope would meet with a contingent of Jewish representatives from various communities around the world. However, the meeting that took place in 1859, four or five months after Edgardo's seizure, quickly dissolved, with the Pope quoted as berating his guests because of their "stirring up [of] a storm all over Europe about this Mortara case." The Pope continued heatedly by saying: "The newspapers can write all they want. I couldn't care less what the world thinks!" These quotes are not very saintly and are questionable translations from the Latin or other language the delegates might have been conversing in. It was reported that he finished his outburst with: "So strong is the pity I have for you, that I pardon you, indeed, I must pardon you." These utterances by the Pope indicate that he was likely feeling attacked by those who had no jurisdiction to meddle in his affairs. On a later occasion, the Pope declared "what I have done for this boy, I had the right and the duty to do. If it happened again, I would do the same thing." And, indeed, a case like Edgardo's was fated to happen again.

There are some major disruptions for which Edgardo's case is cited as a contributing factor. During this period, the Papal State was only standing in the way of the Italian Unification military by the grace of the Austrian and French garrisons. The sentiment of a unified Italy was strong both from inside and outside the prospective borders of the region. Napoleon III, leader of France, had been supporting the Pope because of his peoples' inclinations, but due to the international pressure the Pope was facing over Edgardo, it was increasingly harder to remain neutral. When another child was ripped from his parents' home by the state, the French military finally had the justification that it needed to pull out of Rome. When that happened, the capital fell to the Unification troops almost immediately. With a new government and courts in place everywhere except for the modern-day Vatican area, there was new hope for the justice that the Mortara family desperately wanted. The inquisitor that had ordered the removal of their son was soon after arrested and put on trial. Unfortunately, after an exhausting trial in which Feletti fought the assumptive authority of the new government and claimed God and the Virgin Mary would be his defence lawyers, he was found innocent. Their reasoning was that Feletti had only been following orders.

Another important occurrence that is attributed to the Mortara case is the widespread Jewish diaspora uniting for a single cause. Dov Levitan, a scholar who was writing on the Edgardo Mortara kidnapping at a later time, noted that "the great sence of Jewish solidarity that emerged in the latter half of the 19th century [as] Jews rose to the cause of their brethren in various parts of the world." There were Jewish councils operating out of the United Kingdom as well as in France and other countries who all began to speak to their needs as a global community. Momolo was supported by these organizations throughout his endeavours to retrieve his child. Without a united front, the global diaspora could advocate for themselves in the face of closeted, political antisemitism. Another scholar, Timothy Verhoeven, suggested that the Mortara's case, "more than any other single issue ... exposed the divide between supporters and opponents of the Vatican." Although there were many other instigating factors in both of these main political changes, historians do still attribute Edgardo Mortara's kidnapping to be one of them.

The Priest

When the capital fell, Edgardo fled the area with the priests he was closest to, but not before seeing his brother in Italian military garb. At first Edgardo yelled: "Get back, Satan!" and when his brother, Riccardo, declared himself as Edgardo's brother, Edgardo refused to speak with him until he "[took] off that assassin's uniform." What transpired at that point is unknown, but it did result in Edgardo's escape from the army's grasp. He took on a fake name and sheltered in Austria. After that, Edgardo quickly rose through the ranks of the Church in France, and became a priest early at the age of 21. The normal age for joining the priesthood is 23, and so the Pope had actually written a recommendation for him in order to push forward in his studies. He received a kind of salary of 7,000 lire in order to fully live out the Church's desires. Allegedly, he became a much in demand priest due to his ability to speak and read many languages. He travelled far and wide to deliver sermons. And he did his best to make up to his family. His father passed away during this time, but he did manage to become close to his mother and some of his siblings. Other relatives of his were far less receptive, but whenever he preached in Italy, many of his family members would come to see his sermons.

When one thinks of kidnapping cases, it is normal to picture tearful reunions or dead loved ones. All to many kidnapping cases today end in sorrow, while still many more finish with parents being able to hold their children, and lovers able to be with their partners again. In this kidnapping case, Edgardo's whereabouts were well known by his parents and by international authorities. It is a different sort of playing field when your government abducts your child. It is this callous way of acting blindly in the name of faith that brought about the notions of church and state being separate entities. Edgardo's family had to fight for every chance with him that they got until he was an adult. Although it is unfortunate that they had to deal with conversion attempts, it is good that they were able to see him flourish in his new life. With a few notable exceptions, his family even seemed to fully support him while still holding to the religion of their ancestors.

What caused Edgardo to remain a devoted Christian instead of going back to his family when he was offered the choice in adulthood, might never be known. However, one only has to look at the antisemitism that was prevalent at the time to understand at least one reason for why he abandoned the faith of his ancestors. Jews across Europe had faced severe discrimination and religious persecution throughout the centuries, right up to the period that Edgardo lived in, as well as directly after his time. Jewish peoples weren't wanted anywhere, and had to put with living in lands where the government believed their faith was a pathway to eternal damnation. When he died in 1940 in Belgium at 88 years old, Nazi Germany had already started their hunt for Jews in that area.

Conclusion

Frightened child or capable adult, Edgardo Mortara and the case of his kidnapping was followed closely around the world. Depending on how close a person was to Italy at the time definitely affected how they might feel about the case. There were instances when interested communities in the United States, for example, were being fed wholly wrong information about the case. With regards to the two narratives being told about his seizure by the state, it seems that regardless of what had been the truth when he was a child, Edgardo had indeed accepted Christianity. After his father died, he continuous urged his mother to convert to Catholicism as well. And despite rumours to the contrary, Marianna passed away as a Jewish woman. Edgardo personally tried to dispel these rumours by saying: "I have always ardently desired that my mother embrace the Catholic faith and I tried many times to get her to do so. However, that never happened."

No matter which narrative is more or less true, the undisputed fact is that both sides used the Mortara case to try and forward their own prerogatives. The Pro-Church side gained both a new conversion and spokesperson for their cause. They were able to use to success of Edgardo Mortara to try and convince practitioners of Judaism that theirs was the only correct path to take. The Unification of Italy's side displayed a broken mother and a disrupted family in order to prove that the Pope was no longer the appropriate authority for ruling the country. Michael Goldfarb, a later scholar, has stated that the incident provided "an embarrassing example of just how out of touch with modern times the Church was [and] Pope Pius IX was incapable of bringing the Church into the modern era." They were able to rip out the old foundations of the Papal States and a divided Italy and place a new king in command of the unified state with international approval. The Mortara family was left divided and largely forgotten by all but Jewish scholars since then.

THE CLEVELAND KIDNAPPINGS

SHAUNA BAILEY

The Cleveland Kidnappings

Ariel Castro kidnapped and imprisoned three girls between the years 2003-2013. He kept all three captive in his house on a residential street in Cleveland, Ohio where he raped and tortured them. Michelle Knight, Amanda Berry and Gina DeJesus were held until May 6, 2013. Berry escaped with her six-year-old daughter and was able to call the police. The other girls were rescued, and Castro was arrested within a matter of hours.

On May 8, 2013, Castro was charged with four counts of kidnapping, and three counts of rape. He eventually pled guilty to 937 criminal counts of rape, kidnapping and aggravated murder as part of a plea bargain to escape the death penalty. He was sentenced to life plus 1000 years without the possibility of parole.

Castro was sent to prison on August 2, 2013, and committed suicide on September 3. He in was found dead in his prison cell. He used his bedsheet to hang himself.

Ariel Castro was born on July 11, 1960, in San Juan, Puerto Rico. When his parents divorced, his mother moved Castro and his three brothers to the United States. They first moved to Reading, Pennsylvania and then to Cleveland. Castro's father and other family members were living there. He graduated from Lincoln-West High School in 1979. Castro worked factory jobs but supplemented his income by playing in a band. He was considered one of the top three Latin bass players in Cleveland.

Castro met Grimilda Figueroa, his future girlfriend, when his family moved across the street from her family's home. Once they were together, the unmarried couple lived with both sets of parents before purchasing the house at 2207 Seymour Avenue in 1992. The house had four bedrooms, one bathroom and an unfinished basement. Not long after moving in Castro started working in the basement. He installed a heavy trapdoor and soundproofed it. Once he was finished, no one was allowed to enter the basement.

After moving into the house. the relationship between Castro and Figueroa began to fall apart. Figueroa's family claims that Castro beat her breaking her nose, ribs and arms. She suffered from a fractured skull after he threw her down a flight of stairs. Castro was arrested for domestic violence but wasn't prosecuted because Figueroa was too afraid to press charges.

Castro began to show dominating behavior, keeping Figueroa a near prisoner in their home. He boarded up all the windows and put multiple locks on the doors. At times, he would padlock the doors from the outside when he left. He might be gone up to four days when he was traveling with his band. Castro installed multiple security alarms and then placed mirrors all over the house until he was certain that nothing could happen in the house without him seeing it.

Castro liked to play power games. He would pretend to leave the house and then sneak back in to monitor the phone from an extension in the basement. If Figueroa called anyone, Castro would beat her. One day Figueroa's sister saw Castro shoving her into a carboard box and closing the lid. He told Figueroa to stay in the box until he gave her permission to get out. The police were called multiple times, and Figueroa was in and out of domestic violence shelters. She always returned claiming she did it for the children.

In 1996, Figueroa and her four children finally moved out of the house. Castro continue to harass and attack Figueroa after she left him. When he found out that she was seeing security guard, Fernando

Colon, Castro was furious. One day when he saw Colon taking his kids to school, Castro tried to run him over. Colon dodged out of the way and was unharmed. Colon pressed charges, but they were dropped due to lack of evidence. Figueroa was given full custody of the children in 1997, and Castro was denied any visitation rights.

In 2005, Figueroa accused Castro of injuring her and trying to abduct his daughters. He broke her nose, dislocated her shoulders and fractured her ribs. He hit her so hard that a blood clot formed in her brain. Figueroa was granted a temporary restraining order against Castro, but it was thrown out a few months later for reasons that are unclear.

Castro began to try to make contact with his teenage daughters. He would show up at their house unannounced or at their school. He gave them money and gifts randomly. He convinced his two youngest daughters to claim Colon sexually abused them. Despite the lack of evidence and testimony in favor of Colon, he was found guilty of four counts of sexual abuse. He was given a few months' probation and had to register as a sex offender. Because of this Colon lost his job and the relationship between him and Figueroa ended. Grimilda Figueroa died in 2012 from a brain tumor. After Castro's conviction in 2013, Colon tried to get the verdict over turned but was denied.

Ariel Castro worked as a bus driver for the Cleveland Metropolitan School District for 22 years. In 2004, he was accused of leaving a student in the bus while he bought lunch. He was suspended for making an illegal turn while having students aboard the bus five years later. In 2012, he was suspended again for using the bus to go shopping. Later that same year, he was fired for leaving the bus unlocked and unattended two blocks from his home.

All three of his victims were young, short in stature with big breasts. They all knew at least one of his children but didn't know Castro personally. They were kidnapped after accepting rides from Castro. He drove them to his house, used an excuse to get them inside and then restrained them. Castro's house on Seymour Street was approximately three miles from the neighborhood where he picked them up.

In August, 2002, Castro kidnapped Michelle Knight who was 20 at the time. He offered her a ride which she accepted because she knew one of Castro's daughters. Castro convinced Knight to come into his house with the promise of a puppy for her son. Once inside, he raped and then imprisoned her. She remained his captive for the next 11 years.

The day that Knight disappeared she was scheduled to appear in court for a child custody case involving her son who was in the custody of the state. The police didn't spend much time investigating her disappearance. At 21 she was an adult, and they thought she had probably left because she was angry over losing custody of her son. Knight was removed from the National Crime Information Center database 15 months after her disappearance. Castro often ridiculed Knight about the fact that "nobody cared" that she was missing. Knight had the hope of seeing her son who was two when she was kidnapped to keep her going.

"I have to live for him. And I'm fighting to stay alive for him."

Amanda Berry was taken the day before her 17th birthday on April 21, 2003. She was last seen leaving her part-time job at Burger King. Castro offered her a ride home. Like Knight, she accepted the ride because she knew Castro's daughter. He lured Berry inside by telling her that his daughter was there. "He wasn't mean in the car. Like, he was talkative and he kept the conversation going and he was talking about his kids and how one of his kids worked at the Burger King that I worked at because I had my uniform on, so he was talking about that for a couple of minutes. I couldn't tell that he was this horrible man talking to him in the van." She was his captive for the next 10 years.

At first the FBI considered Berry a runaway. It took a week and a phone call before the disappearance was classified as a kidnapping.

A week after her daughter went missing her mother, Louwana Miller, received a call from an unidentified male, using Berry's phone. He said, "I have Amanda. She's fine and will be coming home in a couple of days." The technology to track cell phones was new, but the call led the FBI within two blocks of Castro's house.

"We spent about a week, around the clock, in that area, hoping that this would world be used again," FBI agent Tim Kolonik said. The phone was never used again.

Castro made Berry an unsettling promise after a few months of her captivity.

"He would always tell me when he got another girl in the house that you know 'I'm just looking for another girl and then I'll take you home,' "Berry revealed.

Castro kept part of his promise, He found another girl, but he didn't let Berry go.

On April 2, 2004, Gina DeJesus, who was 14 at the time, disappeared. DeJesus and Ariel Castro's daughter, Arlene were walking home from Willow Wright Middle School. They stopped at a pay phone to call Grimilda Figueroa, Castro's ex-wife to see if Arlene could stay at DeJesus's house. When Figueroa refused, the girls parted ways. Arlene Castro was the last person to see Gina DeJesus before her disappearance.

Castro asked DeJesus to help him find Arlene. DeJesus got into his car because he was Arlene's father, and he also played in her father's band. Castro drove around for a while simply talking to DeJesus. "I was kind of freaking out a little bit when he didn't turn around, but then when he started talking to me about his daughter and how he was going to take his daughter to the mall and stuff, I kind of, I little bit relaxed, but not really because I was still a little scared". Castro then used the pretense of needing help moving a speaker to get her inside the house. Never suspecting any the danger, DeJesus agreed to help him. He got her to go down into the basement by telling her that was a way to exit the house. She was also his captive for 10 years. Castro is on video attending vigils for DeJesus. He offered his support to her family, and posted "Missing" fliers.

Castro thought that the security camera at the school had recorded the kidnapping of DeJesus. He didn't know it wasn't working at the time. He became paranoid about being caught. He wrote a four-page long confession/suicide note. He wrote about his childhood, his relationship with Grimilda Figueroa and gave the reasons he was keeping the women captive. In the letter, Castro lied. He claimed that he and Figueroa were married, and he had never hit her except in self-defense. He claimed that Knight, Berry, and DeJesus were with him voluntarily, and he paid them to have sex. Then he wrote they were there against their will, but that they were responsible because they had made the decision to get in his car. Nine years later, Castro's note was discovered in a kitchen drawer by the police after the women had escaped.

The kidnappings of Berry and DeJesus received media attention throughout the years. They were featured on a segment of *America's Most Wanted* in 2004. The segment was re-aired several times in the next few years. Their stories were linked together almost immediately since they both disappeared from nearly the same spot. They were profiled on the *Oprah Winfrey Show* and on the *Montel Williams Show*. It was on the *Montel Williams Show* in 2004 that Sylvia Browne, a self-proclaimed psychic, told Berry's mother that her daughter was dead, and that she was "in water." Devastated, Louwana Miller took down all of Berry's pictures and gave away her possessions. Despite what she was told by the psychic, Miller never stopped hoping her daughter would come home abd kept Berry's name in the press year after year until her death in 2006 of heart failure. Dejesus's family stayed active in the search for Gina. "Every year there was a vigil for Gina. There were memorials outside the house. We were living every day in the hope she would come home...," DeJesus's cousin reported.

When Castro kidnapped Knight, he took her upstairs, raped her and then tied her up. He left her there for three days before he came in and fed her.

A day after she was abducted, Castro raped Berry and then forced her to shower with him. Then he chained her to a pole in the basement.

Castro kept DeJesus for a month before he raped her. Even though she was a virgin she knew it was going to happen. She just didn't know when. He raped her on May 7, 2004. "We gotta celebrate. That was your first time," Castro told her as he got dressed after he was finished with her.

That was just the beginning for the three women. During their captivity, Knight, Berry, and DeJesus were physically, sexually, and psychologically abused. The women lived in constant fear. According to Berry, "...every day was unpredictable because you never knew how he was going to act." If his captives disobeyed him in any way, they were brutally beaten, starved, and threatened to be killed with a gun that he carried with him.

At first Castro kept each woman in the sound proofed basement. He restrained them with duct tape, gagged them and chained them to a pole with a bike helmet covering their head. Once he decided that they could be "trusted" they were imprisoned upstairs in the second floor bedrooms.

The women were placed in separate bedrooms and chained at the waist to the radiator by a five foot length of heavy chain. Berry explained the emotion of being chained very simply. "Five feet had become my whole world."

They were forced to use plastic buckets as toilets that weren't emptied very often. If Castro fed them at all, they were given one meal a day, cold fast food or a bag of chips. He often starved them for days at a time. The women were allowed to shower once or twice a week. They were given Castro's old clothes to wear.

The door knobs were removed and the bedroom doors were kept padlocked. There was a hole cut in each one so that Castro could spy on them. The bedroom windows were boarded shut from the inside. At some point he placed gates between the doors. The women could talk to each other. They were able interact at times, but if he thought they were being too friendly with each other he punished them.

The women reported that they were raped up to five times a day. It was the only time the chains were removed. Castro made them tell him how much they wanted him and how sexy he was. If they refused to tell him what he wanted to hear, he hurt them more. He paid the women after raping them to make the sex seem more consensual. They could exchange the money for certain things in a type of weird barter system.

Knight and DeJesus spent several years chained together. He raped them while they were in the same be together. DeJesus said she would cry as she rolled away so she didn't have to watch. After he was finished with Knight, he raped Dejesus next. Knight would often hold her hand to give her a tiny bit of comfort.

Knight was impregnated by Castro at least five time. She miscarried every time. Each time he realized she was pregnant, Castro would beat Knight with dumbbells, punch, kick, slam her against the walls or starve her. She was beaten so badly that she lost her hearing in one ear and was partially blind in one eye.

If he allowed the women to go into the backyard, they had to wear sunglasses and wigs and were instructed to keep their heads down.

Castro loved to play mind games with the women. Several times he made DeJesus play Russian Roulette with him. He forced them to watch *America's Most Wanted*. It was about Berry's and DeJesus's disappearances, and they had to watch as their families were interviewed. Berry watched her mother on TV as Miller begged her to come home. Watching her mother made Berry determined to survive.

"That kept me going. And I said I'm going to make it home to you as long as you fight, I'm going to fight."

Berry saw the *Montel Williams Show* where the psychic told her mother that her daughter was dead. She was outraged and heartbroken over her mother's grief. Berry found out about her mother's death in 2006 from a TV report. Castro got took pleasure from making them watch reports of their kidnappings and interviews with their family members. He especially liked knowing that as the families appealed to the public for help that he was keeping the women about three miles from their homes.

Castro pretended to leave and would then wait outside to test them. He wanted to see if they would try to escape. Sometimes he would hide and as they got close to the open door he would slam in shut in their faces. He often made jokes about the book deals the could have after they were free.

Castro didn't like it when Knight, Berry and DeJesus became too close. He deprived and rewarded the girls to keep them apart. He would give one a little more food, another a little less or he might give one different clothes. "It was just simple things, but when you don't have anything, you're like 'Well, why don't I have that. I want that,'" DeJesus explained.

During the time that the women were kept captive Castro had visitors. When his daughter Arlene visited, he moved all three women into the basement and chained them to a pole. They were able to hear as Castro and Arlene talked and laughed. He left them in the basement for four days. If they had yelled, Arlene would have been able to hear them. They didn't make any noise. They didn't because they didn't want to take the chance that he'd kill one or all of them.

When another daughter visited hid them in his van which was parked in the garage. They were chained to the bottom of the seats. They spent two days in the hot car with no food or water.

Anthony Castro, Ariel's son described what it was like inside his father's house. "The house was always locked. There were places we could never go. There were locks on the basement. Locks on the garage.

There were several times that the women were seen or heard and had the chance of being discovered which would have led to their rescue sooner. In 2004, the police go to Castro's house to investigate the allegation that he left a child unattended on his bus. No one answered the door. After speaking to Castro later, the police determined that no crime had been committed. He had Knight and Berry imprisoned in the house. In November,2011, a neighbor's sister saw a woman with a baby banging on an upstairs window. The police responded to the call, but after walking around the house they left. In 2012, another neighbor, Elsie Cintron contacted the police after her daughter saw a naked woman in the backyard. It is unclear whether or not the police responded to this call. Four women who were out for a walk saw three naked women with dong chains and leashes around their necks in the backyard. They called the police. The women waited for hours but the police never showed. All three women were captives all of these times.

At some point. Castro began to favor Berry, telling the other two women that she was his new wife. He began raping Knight and DeJesus in the backyard instead of inside the house. There were some of Castro's neighbors who say the women chained outside the house, but none of them called the police.

Berry became pregnant in 2007. Castro did not try to make her miscarry as he had with Knight. He actually forced Knight to miscarry while Berry was pregnant. He didn't rape her and made sure that she was given enough to eat to carry the baby to full term. At first, he planned to leave the baby at a church after it was born. Sometime during the pregnancy his attitude changed and Castro became excited about being a father again. Berry went into labor on Christmas Day, He took her and Knight into the basement where he had placed a child's inflatable pool. He told Knight to help deliver the baby and threatened to kill her if the baby died. When Berry's baby girl was born, Knight had to preform CPR to resuscitate her. There were no other problems after that. Berry named the little girl Jocelyn. Jocelyn was left in the bedroom with Berry. Castro removed Berry's chain. Castro didn't provide any necessities for the baby so the women used old clothes and sewed clothes for Jocelyn.

According to Berry, Castro changed after Jocelyn was born. He became a different person around the little girl. He loved his daughter and she loved him. When Jocelyn became a toddler, and was more aware of her surroundings, Castro began to call Knight, Juju, and Dejesus was called Chelsea. He didn't want the little girl to know Knight's and DeJesus's real names so if she mentioned them in public no one would make the connection with the missing women. He allowed Berry to use her real name. He removed their chains when Jocelyn began to notice and ask questions. Castro allowed them to move around inside the house under his supervision. He kept a gun visible at his waist at all times. Jocelyn was about four when Castro began taking her out of the house. She called him "daddy" and he took her to visit his mother who she called "grandma." He took her to church and allowed her to go outdoors and play. At times, he would introduce her as his granddaughter. When he showed one of his daughters pictures of the little girl he claimed she was his girlfriend's daughter. Once the women were released, DNA tests confirmed that Castro was Jocelyn's biological father.

On May 6, 2013, Ariel Castro left the house and forgot to lock the heavy outside door. Six-year-old Jocelyn was the one who brought it to her mother's attention. Berry didn't try to break through the bolted storm door. She thought Castro may have been testing them as he had before. When Berry saw the neighbors through the screen, she began to scream for help. Angel Cordero, Castro's neighbor, responded to Berry's cries for help. He spoke very little English so he wasn't able to communicate with her. Another neighbor, Charles Ramsey, joined

Cordero and began to kick through the bottom of the storm door. Berry crawled out with her daughter. She told Ramsey she, her daughter and two other women were being kept in the house against their will. Berry went to another neighbor's house and called 911.

Her words to the operator were, "Help me. I'm Amanda Berry. I've been Kidnapped and I've been missing for 10 years. And I'm here. I'm free now."

Knight and DeJesus refused to leave the house fearing Castro's reaction if they were caught because they thought he was testing them again. When the responding Cleveland police officers walked through the upstairs hall way, Knight and DeJesus came out, finally convinced they were being rescued. Knight, Berry, DeJesus and Jocelyn were taken to MetroHealth Medical Center. Berry, DeJesus, and Jocelyn were released the next day. Knight wasn't released until four days after.

On the same day that the women were rescued, Castro was pulled over and arrested in a parking lot. His two brothers were with him and were arrested as well. Initially, the press reported that all three brothers were suspects in the abductions. Castro confessed to his crimes and convinced the police that his brothers had no part in the kidnappings. They were released the next day.

Most of his neighbors and other people who knew Castro were shocked by the story the women told. Castro had been very clever and very smooth about keeping the women hidden. His house was really visible when you walked past it. He had disguised the boarded up windows which he had covered with quilts because he always kept the curtains closed. He didn't keep his yard in perfect condition but it was never bad enough to draw attention from anyone. He said hello and talked to his neighbors. No one suspected Castro had a double life and that when he was behind closed doors he became a totally different person: a sadistic and violent on.

On May 8, Castro was charged with four counts of kidnapping and three counts of rape. These charges carried a prison sentence of 10 years to life in Ohio.

On May 9, he had his first court appearance in Cleveland Municipal Court. His bail was set at $8,000,000—$2,000,000 for each kidnapping charge. He was also facing aggravated murder charges for his role in Knight's miscarriages and a kidnapping charge for each day each woman was held. Castro's attorneys said he would plead "not guilty" to all the charges of kidnapping and rape.

On June 7, Cuyhoga County grand jury indicted Castro on 329 counts, plus 2 counts of aggravated murder. The indictments only covered the period from August, 2002 to February, 2007. The county prosecutor Timothy J. McGinty said the investigation was ongoing and any other findings would be presented to the grand jury, Since Castro was found competent to stand trial, McGinty planned on pursuing the death penalty once the case went to trial.

On June 12, Castro entered a not guilty plea. Craig Weintraub said, "It is our hope that we can continue to work toward a resolution to avoid having an unnecessary trial about aggravated murder and the death penalty. We are sensitive to the emotional strain and impact that a trial would have on the women, their families, and the community."

On July 12, the grand jury returned with indictment for the time Castro held the women from early 2007 until their release in 2013, These new indictments brought his total to 977 counts: 542 counts of kidnapping, 2 counts of aggravated murder and one possession on criminal tools. Castro pled not guilty to the new indictments.

On July 26, Castro pled guilty to 957 of the 977 charges against him. These included kidnapping, rape and aggravated murder charges. His guilty plea was part of a plea bargain where Castro would server consecutive life sentences in prison plus 1000 years without the possibility of parole. He had to forfeit his assets including his home which would be demolished.

The law firm representing the three women released a statement after the plea bargain was accepted. "The women are relieved by today's plea. They are satisfied by this resolution to the case and are looking forward to having these legal proceedings draw to a final close in the near future."

The sentencing hearing was on August 1, 2013. Michelle Knight was the only victim to appear in court. Amanda Berry and Gina DeJesus sent someone else to read their victim's impact statements.

Castro addressed the court for 20 minutes before his sentencing. "To clear the record, I am not a monster, I did not prey on these women, I just acted on my sexual instincts because of my sexual addiction," Castro said. "As God is my witness, I never beat these women like they're trying to say I did. I never tortured them." He went on to explain he was addicted to pornography and sex. He said the accusations that he had beat and tortured the women were false. He claimed most of the sex had been consensual.

He shifted from being apologetic to blaming the FBI for not catching him. He told them that if they had checked the security tape from the school that they would have caught him 10 years earlier. Next, he blamed his victims, saying they were not virgins when he had sex with them. He shifted back to apologetic when he said, "I hope they can find in their hearts to forgive me because we had a lot of harmony going on in that home."

Knight read her statement and told Castro, "You took 11 years of my life away. I spent 11 years in hell, now your hell is just beginning. I will overcome all that has happened, but you will face hell for eternity. I will live on, you will die a little every day as you think of the 11 years of atrocities that in inflicted on us. I can forgive you, but I will never forget."

The house at 2007 Seymour Avenue where he had held the women was demolished on August 7, 2013, as part of his plea agreement. Knight walked through the crowd that had gathered and hand out yellow balloons which she said represented missing children. The balloons were released just before the demolition began.

One month into his prison sentence, on October 10, 2013, Ariel Castro committed suicide. He was found hanging by a bedsheet in his cell at the Correctional Reception Center in the Pickaway Correctional Institution. The staff performed CPR before he was taken to the Ohio State University Wexner Medical Center in Columbus Ohio. He was pronounced dead shortly after arrival. The following day an autopsy was performed. The Franklin County coroner announced the cause of death was suicide by hanging

A final report was released on December 3, 2013, that officially concluded that "all available evidence pointed to suicide including a shrine-like arrangement of family pictures and a Bible in Castro's cell, an increasing tone of frustration in his prison journal and the reality of spending the rest of his life in prison while subject to constant harassment."

Michelle Knight, Amanda Berry and Jocelyn and Gina DeJesus once freed had to learn to live in the real world again. They had to heal and find a way to move past the 11 years of imprisonment. Now the three women have the freedom to make choices for themselves.

THE KIDNAPPING OF BOBBY GREENLEASE

NATHAN NIXON

The Bobby Greenlease Kidnapping

The story of Bobby Greenlease is that of a tragedy. This young boy was taken from the one place a child should always feel safe; a school. The heart of the collective world was shattered while witnessing the terrible, sickening events that were unfolding. Only monsters could do such terrible things. Who would do this? How could someone stoop to this level? Most importantly, why would someone resort to this? In 1950's rural America, crimes like this just didn't happen. The turmoil that would ensue after this horrible act is one of confusion, betrayal, and heart sinking results. An innocent boy was gone much too soon, and two senseless criminals were gone much too late.

The day was September 28, 1953. A school for small children in Kansas City, Missouri was having a normal day. Classrooms were filled with young children learning the basics for their futures. Children filed in by the dozens, eagerly greeted by the smiling, caring faces of the teachers they all had learned to trust and love. This was the essence of the French Institute of Notre Dame De Sion. This was the place of learning for six year old Bobby Greenlease.

In 1953, the level of school security was vastly lower than it is today. Teachers and administration alike were much more trusting of the adults that would interact on a daily basis with children. When a mysterious woman came through the front door of the school at 10:55 A.M. that morning, there was little more than a few questions of her intentions. This mystery woman explained that she was there to pick up Robert Cosgrove Greenlease Jr. In the routine of any school, teachers and office personnel quickly learn the family and caregivers of each of their students. Needless to say, there was some suspicion of this woman who had never before been through the doors of this school and most certainly had never had any interactions with Bobby Greenlease.

The mystery woman was very anxious. She was described later as "fidgety and nervous" by school personnel. She told them that the situation was dire. She explained that she was Bobby's aunt and that his mother had suffered a catastrophic heart attack. Bobby's mother was in the hospital and he needed to come with her at once. While the school personnel were quite suspicious, it was Bobby who quelled their worry. Bobby was pulled from class at approximately 11:05 A.M. and brought to the front of the school. The mystery woman got down on a knee in front of Bobby and quickly explained that he needed to come with her.

The innocence of Bobby Greenlease is ultimately what this woman was able to take advantage of. Bobby was a trusting little boy. He learned from his daily interactions to listen to the adults around him. His parents would later explain how he was such an easygoing little boy who never gave them problems. He was described by his teacher as happy and always striving to please. For Bobby, when an adult told him to do something, he did it. He trusted them, and he had learned at a young age that he was to do as he was told. Little Bobby Greenlease always did what he was told, and he always did it with a beautiful, contagious smile on his face.

Bobby took the hand of this mysterious woman quickly after she explained what had happened. The worries of school personnel were quelled by seeing the reaction of Bobby. Surely, they thought, he wouldn't seem so eager to go with this woman if he didn't know her. With that, Bobby Greenlease left the French Institute of Notre Dame De Sion with his "aunt." Sister Moreland later recalled that "Bobby went to her with no hesitation. As they walked out of the front door, she had one arm around his shoulder and the other one holding his hand. They entered into an awaiting taxi cab. Bobby showed no fear or withdrawal from her. Everything appeared as normal."

At around 11:30 A.M. a school official, Sister Marthanna, called the Greenlease home to learn the condition of Mrs. Greenlease. To her surprise, Mrs. Greenlease answered the phone. The conversation quickly alerted the school that the story was false. Mrs. Greenlease was terrified and immediately called her husband, Robert Cosgrove Greenlease Sr. As he rushed home from work, Mrs. Greenlease alerted the Kansas City police chief. The police chief alerted the FBI of the matter. In the span of just thirty minutes, it was clear that little Bobby Greenlease, full trusting and carrying the innocence that any six year old boy would, had been kidnapped by a mystery woman. A tragedy of epic proportions was unfolding. The events of this day would go on to grip the nation in a sickening, winding road of horror and greed. The investigation was on. The Greenlease family would not have to wait long for answers.

Being as the woman who had left with Bobby had entered a cab, the first job of investigators was to track down the cab driver. Later in the day, police tracked down Willard Pearson Creech. He was a cab driver working for the Toedman Cab Company of Kansas City, Missouri. He was fully compliant with police. He informed investigators that just before 11:00 A.M. a woman entered into his cab asking to be taken to the French Institute of Notre Dame De Sion. The description Creech gave fit that of the woman who had taken Bobby Greenlease. Before the woman exited the cab, she instructed Creech to wait for her outside the school. She had said that she also needed to be taken to the Katz Drug Store at Main and Westport in Kansas City. According to Willard, it was approximately 11 minutes later that the woman came out of the school with the young boy. The boy fit the description of Bobby Greenlease. The last time that Willard Pearson Creech saw the pair, they had stopped in the rear of an early 1950's blue Sedan with Kansas license plates.

The question that was being asked by everyone was why? Why would someone kidnap an innocent six year old boy? How could someone take a child from their school? These questions would be answered very quickly. What happens next sends a chill throughout the Greenlease household.

The first ransom letter arrives just hours after the kidnapping of Bobby. The Greenleases received a letter that was postmarked 6:00 P.M. and designated for special delivery. The letter made the intentions of the kidnappers apparent. The letter stated the demand of $600,000 to be placed in a duffle bag with no bills larger than $20. The ransom would be the largest, for that time, in the history of the United States. The kidnappers ended the letter by promising the safe return of Bobby Greenlease within just 24 hours. This was contingent upon receiving all of the demanded ransom money with no sneaky tricks attempted by investigators. This was the first of many ransom contacts by the kidnappers. Investigators say they received as many as six ransom letters and 15 phone calls. The next ransom letter, however, proved to be even more chilling than the first.

The next communication between the kidnappers and the Greenleases was a letter sent on September 29, 1953. It was postmarked 9:30 P.M. and again sent special delivery. The letter, however, accompanied the Jerusalem medal of which Bobby always wore. This terrified Bobby's parents. The letter again called for $600,000 to be given for the safe return of little Bobby. The kidnappers said that "Bobby was safe, but was becoming quite homesick and wanted to see his mommy."

Within days, the story of Bobby Greenlease had attracted national media attention. The nation collectively shared the grief of the Greenlease family and hoped wholeheartedly for the safe return of Bobby. People could not understand how someone could bring themselves to take a little boy from his school. Moreover, people could not wrap their minds around how the school could let this happen. How could a six year old boy be allowed to leave with a stranger of which the school had never seen before? Many more questions would be asked. The frightening answers would soon rise to the forefront of an investigation that had only just begun.

The final communication from the kidnappers was a phone call at 1:00 A.M. on October 5, 1953. The call came directly to the Greenlease residence. The kidnappers assured the family that Bobby was safe. They stated that they had received the ransom money and that Bobby would be released within 24 hours. This was the last time that the Greenleases would hear any correspondence from the kidnappers.

Carl Hall and Bonnie Heady never had any intentions to return Bobby Greenlease to his family. The grim details of the events that took place would soon be uncovered.

Bonnie Heady was they "mystery woman" who took Bobby Greenlease from Notre Dame De Sion. She had taken Bobby, by taxi, for a few miles where they would meet up with Carl Austin Hall. Bonnie and Bobby would get into a Plymouth station wagon with Carl where they traveled to Johnson County, Kansas. It was here where authorities say Carl Hall shot little Bobby Greenlease to death with a Smith and Wesson .38 caliber revolver.

Robert Cosgrove Greenlease Sr. paid the ransom money in full to the kidnappers. They were completely unaware that Bobby had been murdered on the day of the abduction. At the time, the $600,000 was the largest ransom ever paid in the United States. Upon receiving the ransom money, Carl Hall and Bonnie Heady drove 380 miles to St. Louis, Missouri. Hall became extremely paranoid all the while. He was certain that authorities were closing in on them. He decided to try to divert attention away from the area.

On October 5, Hall purchased a pair of metal suitcases to store the ransom money. He left the duffle bag in an ash pit near St. Louis. Hall had an apartment he had rented in St. Louis on Arsenal Street. In the late hours of October 5, Carl and Bonnie arrived at the apartment.

It is important to note that Bonnie Heady and Carl Hall were heavy drug and alcohol abusers. While not the only motive for the crime, it would explain the unthinkable acts committed by the pair of criminals. Bonnie Heady was a heavy heroin user. Carl Hall would take advantage of this for his own attempted escape.

When Hall and Heady arrived at his apartment, Bonnie was heavily intoxicated. Within minutes, she had fallen asleep in the apartment. This was exactly what Carl had wanted to happen. As soon as she was asleep, Carl took the ransom money and left. He had left his accomplice to the murder of Bobby Greenlease with just $2,000 of the ransom money. He placed the money in her purse and bolted out of the door. The pair had separated on October 5, 1953.

On October 6, Hall went to a local hardware store where he purchased two garbage cans and a shovel. Growing increasingly suspicious of authorities finding out who he was and tracking him down, he acquired a rental car that morning. He drove to the Meramec River in St. Louis County and anxiously looked for a suitable place to bury the ransom money. This proved unsuccessful. He ditched the empty garbage cans and made his way back to the Coral Courts Motel, where he had been staying. By this time the paranoia of Hall was destroying his mind. He became suspicious of other motel patrons that afternoon, and decided to leave the hotel and get a room at the Townhouse Hotel in St. Louis. This would prove costly.

On the afternoon of October 6 at approximately 3:30 P.M. St. Louis police received a call from John Oliver Hager. Hager was a driver for the Ace Cab Company in St. Louis. His information led to the arrest of Carl Hall on the evening of October 6, 1953 at the Townhouse Hotel where he had checked in earlier in the day. Had Hall stayed put at the Coral Courts Motel, he may have never been discovered by Hager. When police arrested Hall, he told them that his name was John James Byrne. This was obviously fictional, but perhaps was a last gasp for freedom. Later on that evening, Hall led police to Arsenal Street to his apartment where Bonnie Heady was staying. Police entered the residence in the late hours of October 6 and arrested Heady. The pair of kidnappers were in police custody.

This began a process of interrogations by the FBI. Hall was interrogated numerous times and put together an illustration of his involvement in the crime. He insisted that all of the $600,000 ransom money was in his possession. Carl Hall admitted to several allegations against him. He admitted to his part in the kidnapping of Bobby. He admitted to actually planning and executing the kidnapping. He also admitted to burying the body of Bobby Greenlease on Heady's property. He even admitted to picking up the ransom money that was set in the requested duffle bag. He did not, however, admit to the actual killing of Bobby Greenlease. This, as he claimed, was carried out by one Tom Marsh.

Carl Hall described a grand scheme that he agreed to with a man named Tom Marsh. He described that, once he and Heady kidnapped Bobby Greenlease, they had given the boy over to Tom Marsh. The couple was to act as the "middle men" in a scheme to extort money from Robert Cosgrove Greenlease Sr. Carl Hall argued that Tom Marsh had killed Bobby, and it was only then that he agreed to bury the body in the shallow grave by the porch of Bonnie Heady's house. The investigators didn't buy it. After more interrogation, Carl reluctantly admitted that he and Bonnie Heady were the only involved parties in the kidnapping and subsequent murder of Bobby Greenlease.

The body of Bobby Greenlease was discovered by police the next day, October 7th, 1953 at 1201 South 38th Street in St. Joseph, Missouri. At approximately 8:40 A.M. police quickly came across the shallow grave while investigating the residence of Bonnie Heady. The body was discovered buried near the front corner of the porch. The little boy's body was wrapped in plastic bags and covered in lime. The Greenlease requested their dentist to positively identify the body. At 1:05 P.M. on October 7, it was officially determined by DNA and dental records to be the body of Robert Cosgrove Greenlease Jr. Bobby's body had been found.

Upon full examination of the house, investigators found heavy blood stains on the basement floor as well as the steps entering the Heady house. Blood stains were also found on two separate fiber rugs as well as a nylon blouse. This gave the indication to police that the body had been moved several times. In addition to the blood stains, several .38 caliber shell casings were found in the house. The FBI criminal investigation lab, after much testing, determined the casings had been fired from a .38 caliber snub nose Smith and Wesson revolver. This same revolver had been found in Carl Hall's possession at the time of his arrest. FBI investigators also determined that a lead bullet found in the floor board of a Plymouth station wagon owned by Bonnie Heady was also fired from the same revolver. They now had hard evidence, along with a near full confession, to indict Carl Hall and Bonnie Heady for the murder of Bobby Greenlease.

It was not until October 11, 1953 that the full story would come out. Carl Hall told investigators the events of Bobby Greenleases murder in full, gruesome detail. He explained that he and Bonnie Heady had taken the victim from Kansas City, Missouri to Overland Park, Kansas. This, he said, was the same day that they had kidnapped Bobby from school. It was a town just outside Kansas City. This is the location where Carl Hall murdered six year old Bobby Greenlease by firing multiple rounds from his .38 caliber Smith and Wesson revolver into the child. Carl Hall then explained that they then transported the body of Bobby 45 minutes away to St. Joseph, Missouri. He then buried the body near the porch in a shallow grave and proceeded to plant flowers on it.

Bonnie Heady subsequently admitted to assisting Carl Hall with the ransom letters. She admitted to providing the instructions of the ransom money drop off to the Greenlease family. She also admitted to being the "mystery woman" who picked up Bobby Greenlease from school on the morning of September 28, 1953. She told investigators of the ruse that she had planned to use to convince school officials into letting her have Bobby.

Carl Hall and Bonnie Heady were tried on October 30, 1953. This was just over a month after their kidnapping and murder of Bobby Greenlease. Judge Albert L. Reeves presided over the case in federal court in St. Louis, Missouri. Both Hall and Heady entered guilty pleas. Shortly after, on November 19, 1953, the jury deliberated for just one hour and eight minutes. They had heard all of the gruesome details of the case. By this time, the nation was gripped on the case. Each day, updates would be put in each city newspaper. Everyone was engulfed in the proceedings. When testimony came out that the couple had planned this disgusting act well in advance, the nation's collective voice screamed for the death penalty. On November 19, 1953, both Carl Hall and Bonnie Heady were recommended for the death penalty by the jury. After just 15 minutes of deliberation by Judge Reeves, he agreed that death by execution fit the crime. Judge Reeves sentenced them both to be executed on December 18, 1953.

"I think the verdict fits the crime," Judge Reeves said. "It is the most coldblooded, brutal murder I have ever tried."

On December 18, 1953, Carl Hall and Bonnie Heady were set to die in the Missouri State Penitentiary in Jefferson City, Missouri. They were executed in the gas chamber. Less than three months after the kidnapping and murder of Bobby Greenlease, Carl Hall was pronounced dead at 12:12 A.M. and Bonnie Heady was pronounced dead just 20 seconds later. A case that gripped a nation was now officially closed.

Officially, only half of the $600,000 ransom was recovered by authorities. In the weeks following the execution, the next step for investigators was to locate the rest of the ransom money. It was determined that the two suitcases which contained the other half of the ransom money were never brought in to the police headquarters at the time of the arrest. While lacking any evidence, the state decided to pursue charges against Lieutenant Louis Ira Shoulders and Patrolman Elmer Dolan. Shoulders was found guilty on April 15, 1954 and subsequently sentenced to three years in federal prison. Elmer Dolan was tried on March 31, 1954. He was also found guilty and sentenced to two years in federal prison. Both men were convicted of perjury. Both men served their sentences, after which they returned to the St. Louis area. Lieutenant Louis Ira Shoulders passed away on May 12, 1962, never having the mistake reconciled. Elmer Dolan was officially pardoned by President Lyndon B. Johnson on July 21, 1965. The lack of evidence against these two men was overlooked, most likely due to circumstance and the relentless effort by the investigation teams to close the case.

The mysterious disappearance of the ransom money has been the source of many myths and conspiracies. To the day, the ransom money has never been recovered. Investigation into a number of conspiracies and theories has turned up no trace of evidence to support them. Perhaps to understand the crime, we must understand who Carl Hall and Bonnie Heady were. To go through with such a horrific act, these two people must have been psychopathic in nature. Their story is one of wonder and disgust, most easily understood by looking at the mental make-up of each and how their paths crossed.

Carl Hall enjoyed great wealth in his childhood. He was the son of a prestigious and wealthy St. Louis lawyer. Hall never had to do any real work for a living. His father passed in 1946, leaving a fortune of $200,000 to his son. Ironically, it was through a heavy drinking habit and drug addiction that he quickly squandered his entire fortune. This would mark the beginning of a downhill spiral for Carl Hall.

Carl Hall had wasted a massive fortune. His drug and alcohol addictions, however, still remained. Upon losing his money, he set out to robbing innocent taxi cab drivers. The epitome of a "five dollars at a time" living, his take was said to be $38 at the time of his capture. He was found guilty of robbery and served 16 months in a state prison, and was released on April 24, 1953. This was a mere five months before his participation in the kidnapping of Bobby Greenlease.

While serving his 16 month sentence at Missouri State Prison, Hall began planning the kidnapping and murder of six year old boy Bobby Greenlease. Bobby was the son of the wealthiest man in Kansas City, Missouri. Robert Cosgrove Greenlease Sr. had gained great wealth as a car dealer. He had gained the bulk of his fortune by introduction General Motors vehicles to the Midwest. The 71 year old also had some family ties to Carl Hall.

As a child, Carl Hall attended military school at the same location as the adopted step-brother of Bobby Greenlease. While they were not friends nor did they even speak to each other, the knowledge of the family was bestowed upon Carl Hall. This would be one more thing to solidify the target of Hall and Heady.

On April 24, 1953, Carl Hall stepped out of prison. He was immediately embraced by a strange woman of whom he had never met before. This woman was Bonnie Brown Heady. She was 41 years old at the time and recently widowed. She was described as a plump, pale woman with a "porcine" face. The mysterious woman kissed Hall on the mouth and held him close. Only after her passionate kissing did she introduce herself to Hall.

Bonnie Brown Heady was a gun smuggler in the 1930's. It was in this line of work she met a bank robber named Dan Heady. Dan was a smuggler, bank robber, and overall low grade criminal of the late 1920's to the 1930's. Dan married Bonnie in 1935. It wasn't long until Dan was arrested for numerous crimes. He attempted to escape from prison to get to his young, red-headed wife Bonnie. He was gunned down by a group of sheriffs before he could fully escape. The story told by the sheriff who shot Dan Heady is a chilling insight into the kind of person that Bonnie was. Upon learning of the shooting and subsequent death of her husband, Bonnie was described as saying "well that's too bad" out of the side of a sly, almost happy grin. It was the lifestyle that Bonnie craved. She was attracted to criminals.

She had heard about who Carl Hall was and the life he lived through many ex-prisoners. She was intrigued. She was addicted to men like Carl Hall and Dan Heady. She was also addicted to heroin and was a heavy alcohol abuser, much like Hall. Upon introduction herself to Carl Hall, she took him to her home in St. Joseph, Missouri. This would prove to be a grim foreshadowing of the events that would take place just over five months down the road.

It is well known that Bonnie Heady was a heavy drinker and heroin addict. Carl Hall was just as guilty as Bonnie was in this regard. They would spend nearly every waking day drinking themselves into a stupor together. When they weren't too drunk to function, they would near overdose on heroin with one another. This engulfed their lives in the 5 months after they had met. This was how they lived their life in Bonnie's home in St. Joseph, Missouri.

It was in the few sober times together that they began to plan the horrific crime they would soon carry out. While Hall had planned out most of the major details while in prison, Heady helped with the finer points of how they would work the ransom and different ways to obtain the ransom without being seen by authorities. When Carl Hall originally proposed she be an accomplice in his terrible plan, Bonnie famously remarked, "Why, that's better than sex!" She had fully agreed to participate.

The night before the duo carried out their kidnapping of Bobby Greenlease, the actions they took part in were a sickening omen. These events were focused on closely in court, as it proved that this was not only a pre-meditated kidnapping, but more importantly it was a pre-meditated murder.

It was pouring down rain the night of September 27, 1953. The couple, wearing heavy boots and rain coats, dug the shallow grave just outside the porch of Bonnie's St. Joseph home. This was the critical piece that allowed jurors to swiftly come to a death sentence after just an hour of deliberation.

The personality that Bonnie Heady and Carl Hall had was on full display in their ransom calls with the Greenleases. The following transcript is one of many, but shows a pattern of the mental games that Hall and Heady were playing with the Greenleases. In the transcript, Hall identifies himself as "M."

Mrs. Greenlease: Hello, this is Mrs. Greenlease.

M: M speaking.

Mrs. Greenlease: We have the money, but we must know that our son is alive and doing well. Could you at least give me that? Can't you give me something that will assure that?

M: That is a reasonable request. To be completely frank with you, this boy is driving us nuts. We couldn't possibly risk taking him to a phone.

Mrs. Greenlease: Well, I can only imagine. Can you do this then? Can you ask him two questions? Give me the answer to the two questions.

M: Well.

Mrs. Greenlease: If I had the answer to these two questions, I would trust and know that my son is alive and well.

M: All right.

Mrs. Greenlease: Ask him the name of our driver in Europe from this summer.

M: All right.

Mrs. Greenlease: The second question is what did you build with the monkey blocks in your playroom the last night you were home with us? If you can get those answers for me, I will feel better and relieved. You know that is the only thing that I want.

M: We have the boy. He is alive and well. Believe me. He is literally driving us crazy.

Mrs. Greenlease: Well I can imagine that. He is a very active little boy.

M: He has been driving us crazy.

Mrs. Greenlease: Could you please get those answers from him?

M: All right.

Bonnie and Carl delighted in these phone calls. The duo deliberately extended the negotiations. They would make several, as many as 15, brief phone calls. Each call would change the plans for the ransom in a way that would extend the process another day. The sadistic cat and mouse game that Hall and Heady were playing with the Greenleases was absolutely sickening. The process was also delayed, moreover, due to the drunkenness of the kidnappers.

Another crucial bit of information was the confession that Carl Hall made about the night he killed Bobby Greenlease. Hall said that he sent Bonnie to take a walk in the field so she didn't have to witness the killing, as well as to keep an eye out for witnesses. It was then that Hall tried to strangle the young boy to death. Even for a six year old boy, Hall said that Bobby was providing strong resistance to this. He was fighting for his life. This actual court record confession from Carl Hall is both chilling and heart breaking.

"I was prepared for that. I had the gun in my coat pocket," Hall said. "I pulled it out and shot once, trying to shoot him in the heart. I had no idea if I had hit him or not, for he was still alive. I shot him through the head on the second shot. I then took him out of the car and laid him there on the ground. I had a plastic bag that I put him in. I remember there being a lot of blood there. This farm, where the killing occurred, is about two miles south and two miles west of the state line."

"I then called on Bonnie to return to the car," Hall continued. "She walked back to the car and help me load the body in the trunk. We drove straight back to her home in St. Joseph. We had to wait until night fall to bury the body; we didn't want the neighbors to see our movements and get suspicious."

When Judge Reeves announced the sentencing, the courtroom broke out into a tearful applause. "I'd rather be dead than poor," Bonnie Heady famously sneered after the sentence announcement. Robert Cosgrove Greenlease Sr. sat through the court proceeding quietly throughout the trial. In the most famous words spoken after the trial from the Greenlease family, he famously said "It's too good for them, but it's the best the law provides."

On September 28, 1953, an innocent boy was taken from his school by sick criminals. An innocent boy was murdered that night by these same sadistic people. Throughout the entire ordeal, the quest for money was a central force in the murder of Bobby Greenlease. Another force, however, was the crazy mental states of a duo of heroin addicts and alcohol abusers who enjoyed the lifestyle. When all was said and done, the entire nation had been taken on an emotional rollercoaster that, sadly, didn't have the happy ending that everyone was hoping for. Instead, a six year old boy was murdered and, although justice was done, it still didn't seem to be enough. For people to deem it a possibility to take a child from school, it doesn't seem that there would ever be a punishment fitting enough to provide the end that was due. From a kidnapping that started on the morning of September 28, 1953, to the gas chamber on December 18, 1953, Bonnie Heady and Carl Hall remained twisted and miserable. All that the Greenlease family could do was wonder what Bobby could have matured into being.

THE MCKAY KIDNAPPING

JAMIE FOSTER

The McKay Kidnapping

The McKay kidnapping is one of Britain's most notorious cases of kidnap and, perhaps, murder. The story itself is interesting enough- it involves mistaken identity, lords and ladies, newspaper magnates and mystery. But the story of how two brothers were punished for the crime, despite a body not having been found (and not ever found to this day), is what sets this case apart.

The two brothers, Arthur and Nizam Hosein, were imprisoned for life because they kidnapped and murdered Lady Muriel McKay. They had not intended to kidnap her; they wanted to kidnap Rupert Murdoch's then wife.

After following the trail back to their farm, officers arrested the pair. But they couldn't find Muriel's body, nor any evidence that she had been murdered. No weapon, no blood; nothing. But that didn't stop prosecutors from pushing ahead with their case against the pair, using damning evidence to send them both to prison for life.

What happened?

The Hosein brothers were born in Dow Village, on the island of Trinidad. They were of Indian heritage, and had family all over the world: some more in the West Indies, some back in India, and many more in England. Their relatives in England had done well for themselves, becoming doctors and lawyers; comparatively, the Hosein brothers were poor.

Arthur Hosein had moved to England to escape poverty in Trinidad and Tobago, and had become a tailor's cutter, like a number of his relatives. He took his brother, Nizam, with him. Nizam was twelve years younger than Arthur, and was in every way the little brother: smaller and quieter. Arthur completed National Service like other British citizens, and eventually settled down with a German woman named Elsa. He was thrown out of the army in 1960, on a dishonorable discharge.

Having settled down in England, the pair decided to buy some land. They bought Rooks Farm on a long term mortgage in 1967, a large farm at 11 acres but in a considerable state of disrepair. The estate was originally built in the seventeenth century, and so required extensive building work to get it into an operational state. For the time being, the two brothers kept pigs and chickens, but this was nowhere near enough to cover their costs. Arthur made trousers as a small side business, as he had learned the tailoring trade from his father.

Arthur, in trying to fit in with his neighbours, wanted to become a local squire and to join in with the regular activities of the town hunt. But not only could he not afford the membership fee, he had no horse- and didn't know how to ride- and he had no guns or riding equipment. His mortgage meant that he was heavily in debt, and he had no way of making a substantial amount of money with the farm in such a terrible state.

Nevertheless, Arthur had pretensions to greatness. In fact, he was known by other locals as 'King Hosein' because of the grand way he would strut about, as if he owned the streets. But neither brother had any pretensions at home as to how they could fund their new life: both knew that they had precious little money. Neither of the brothers could see a way out.

In order to fund this new lifestyle, the brothers decided to take radical action. Watching TV one night, they saw a British TV presenter, David Frost, interviewing Rupert Murdoch. They suddenly realised- if only they could have just a tiny fraction of his fortune, all their problems would be solved. They hatched a plan to kidnap his wife, and demand what to him would be a relatively small ransom. But to the Hosein brothers, it would be enough to completely renovate their farm and live a lavish lifestyle.

Having seen Rupert Murdoch's car on TV, they tracked him down to the suburb of London in which he lived, following his car to his home in Wimbledon. It was December 29th, 1969 when they struck. They followed the car home one last time, before breaking into the house and abducting the woman they found there. But what the brothers didn't account for was that they had kidnapped the wrong woman.

Rather than taking Rupert Murdoch's wife, they had kidnapped a woman named Lady Muriel McKay, the wife of the wealthy baron Lord McKay. Rupert and his wife were on holiday in Australia at the time- the two are Australian, and spent plenty of time in their home country- and the house had been looked after by two of their friends. Muriel McKay was the wide of the deputy chairman of Murdoch's business empire, and the pair of them had been housesitting for him while he was away. They had even used Rupert's car for errands, hence the brothers' confusion.

Alick McKay, Muriel's husband and Rupert's deputy, came home that night at 7:45pm. He found that the telephone had been ripped from the wall, the furniture was scattered and in disarray, and the contents of his wife's handbag had been left strewn across the stairs. In a state of panic, he left the house and frantically called on his neighbor; he called the police from their house at around 8pm that night. Nobody had seen anybody suspicious, and no clues had been left behind as to who had taken his wife.

At 1am the following morning, Alick received a phone call. It was Arthur Hosein- although, of course, Alick didn't know who that was. The man at the other end of the call wouldn't answer any of Alick's questions, but what he did say was the he and his accomplice demanded £1 million. He identified himself as belonging to the M3 Mafia, although neither Alick nor the police knew who that could be, nor what their motivation was.

The police advised Alick not to give in. Normally, during a hostage situation, the kidnapper will state their demands clearly: that they be taken into custody but not face extradition, or that they be allowed to leave the country, or to have so-and-so released from prison. But not 'M3'. The only thing that he ever said he wanted was money; so the police advised Alick not to give in. Besides, the kidnappers seemed unprofessional, even opportunistic.

Over the next few weeks, Alick received at least 18 phone calls from Arthur Hosein, repeating his demand for money and threatening to kill Muriel. Alick also received letters from both Arthur and his wife, including one where the kidnappers seemed to recognise their mistake: "We tried to get Rupert Murdoch's wife. We couldn't get her so we took yours instead. You have a million by Wednesday night or we will kill her."

The letters that Alick received from his wife were even more disturbing. They were most likely written under duress, a fact which didn't elude the police, or Alick. One of them read: "Please do something to get me home. What have I done to deserve this treatment?" Clearly Muriel was being mistreated, and knowing that, Alick knew that he had to get her back.

The investigation was one of the largest undertaken by Scotland Yard up to that point. At the same time, Alick and the rest of their family appealed to the kidnappers on national television to try and get Muriel back. But nothing would shift their resolve. On New Year's Day, the kidnappers called back- but their response did nothing to calm Muriel's family. They stated again that they would accept nothing but a million pounds.

In his desperation to find his wife, Alick contacted an old family friend named Eric Cutler. Alick asked Cutler to fly to Utrecht, a city in the Netherlands, to consult with a Dutch clairvoyant in the hope that he could give some clue as to where Muriel might be. That clairvoyant's name was Gerard Croiset, and he told Cutler that Muriel was being held in a white farmhouse, somewhere to the north of London. The bad news was that if she wasn't found within 14 days, she would be never be seen again.

The end game

Alick and the rest of Muriel's family were becoming increasingly desperate to find her. Time and time again they were called by the kidnappers, but whenever they were asked how exactly they wanted the money to be delivered, they would hang up. This puzzling behavior only made Alick's confusion and sadness worse, because there seemed to be no way he could get his wife back.

Meanwhile, police continued to search. They searched in and around London, both in the city and in the countryside, but no trace of either Muriel or her kidnappers could be found. As part of their attempts to bring the kidnappers to reason, the police had the McKay family doctor appear on TV. He said that Muriel needed medication, without which she could die; perhaps it was this that finally made the kidnappers flinch.

On February 1st, just over a month after Muriel had been kidnapped, Ian McKay received a phone call. The kidnappers told him to bring just £500,000 to a crossroads, and leave it there, and that he would then be given further instructions on how to get his mother back. Taking advantage of the situation, a policeman went along instead of Ian, but the kidnappers either saw or sensed the ambush and never arrived.

On February 6th, Ian received another call. This time, the kidnappers told him that they would only meet with Alick and his daughter, who were told to deliver two suitcases full of cash to another location. This time, they would take the Tube to a station called Epping, just on the outskirts of London. They were then to take a taxi to a nearby small town called Bishop's Stortford, and leave the two suitcases opposite a minivan near a garage. Again, two policemen went instead of the McKay's. They left the suitcases where they had been told- and waited.

They didn't have to wait long. A small Volvo was driven repeatedly past the cases, up and down. He came by four or five times, and the police officer on lookout took the car's licence plate registration. After some time, two members of the public actually noticed the case, and called the local police, who promptly arrived to take the suitcases to the police station. But the car's number plate was enough for officers to track him down: they found the car at Arthur Hosein's farm not far away, only a few miles down the road. Officers made a house call the next day, with a search warrant to try and find Mrs McKay's stolen jewellery.

They didn't find much. The brothers' possessions were few: an empty Elastoplast tin, an empty cigarette packet, some paper flowers and a billhook. A billhook is an implement commonly found on farms that looks like a scythe. The brothers had also lent a billhook from another nearby farm not long before. But the fingerprints that police were able to take from the brothers' house matched the fingerprints found on the ransom notes. It was a certainty that Arthur and his brother had been the two men behind this horrible episode.

But what police didn't understand was this: Muriel was nowhere to be found. Her body was not at the Hoseins' house, nor did it seem to have been buried anywhere on the farm. Not only could they not find her body, but there had been no sign of a struggle, no physical evidence like clothing or her handbag- not a trace of Muriel McKay. Nevertheless, the two brothers were taken into custody and charged with murder.

The Trial

The pair were intensely interrogated, and they did all but confess. During his interrogation, Nizam was shown the billhook that police alleged was the murder weapon. He started to shake, and didn't dare look at it. After being shown the twine, he shook his head, and began to cry, shouting: 'Let me die! Let me die!'

Whatever happened to Lady Muriel McKay, the police couldn't tell. They couldn't find her body, nor could they get any meaningful confession out of either of the brothers. But that didn't stop them from pushing ahead with the trial. The pair were tried at England's most famous court, the Old Bailey, on a charge of kidnap and murder. Incredibly, the two brothers blamed one another for having killed Muriel. But neither would confess.

Arthur Hosein's cross-examination was the most interesting. He took to the stand in different attire each day. His first day in the dock, he wore a black, single breasted dinner suit, with a black bow tie, and a shirt with a black collar and white polka dots. Apparently, Arthur owned over fifty suits such as these, which he perhaps made himself.

Arthur was clear: he had nothing to do with the dreadful crime that had been committed. He described the day of the 29th as that like any other. His usual schedule ran like this: waking between 11 and 12 noon, while Nizam tends to the animals; running errands, and relaxing in the evening. On that day, he said, he had a terrible cold because of a flu epidemic which had been raging in the area. He went to a neighbor's farm to buy a calf, because the family bought milk by bulk, and had too much.

That evening, he spoke to a friend on the telephone, ate, had coffee and biscuits, and went to bed at 7.30pm- quite early. He denied making the calls received by the McKay family that night, after midnight. He also denied calling the family between about 10 and 11pm two nights later, and insisted that he had been visiting another tailor that day. According to Arthur, he and his brother had been out in the early evening, when Nizam had gone to the pub to buy Arthur some cigarettes, and not returned. Assuming he had met his girlfriend, Arthur carried on home without him. He insisted that he was at home watching the news at the time of the botched ransom drop-off that evening.

Of that night, Arthur said that he had a drink in the lounge, and watched the news, waiting for his brother. He returned at midnight, drenched through by rain. Arthur told the court: "He is twelve years my junior, a stranger in a strange land. My duty is to protect him. I didn't want to provoke him, but all the while, I had considerable concern about him in this country."

During his time in the witness box, Arthur was handed the first and second billhooks, either of which the prosecution thought could have been the murder weapon. Handling it, Arthur appeared calm- completely unlike his brother, whose outburst during his interrogation had led the police to believe they had the right men. Mr Hudson, the prosecutor, asked him: "Do you use a billhook?" To which Arthur responded, almost cryptically: "A calf died through mishandling. We were going to bury it." At that point, the judge asked, "Did you chop the calf up?" To which Arthur replied "I instructed my brother to."

Hudson's point in all of this was that he believed the brothers to have killed Muriel with the billhook, before feeding her body to their dogs. This could be the only explanation for why no trace of her could be found. The judge asked Arthur, "Was it [the calf] fed to the dogs?", and Arthur responded "I believe so." Arthur entirely denied ever having met, seen or even heard of Muriel, and categorically stated that she had never been at the farm. And forensic evidence agreed with him, since nobody had been able to find a single shred of evidence to suggest that she had been.

During his last moments on the witness stand, Arthur took the opportunity to address the court. He told them, and the jury: "Believe me, I have great sympathy for the McKay family. I have a mother myself. I am no murderer even if I am found guilty. These hands... [at which point he held out his hands] ...are artistic, not destructive. I believe in the preservation of Man. That is what I am living for."

After this point, a forensic expert was called to the stand. He told the court that while he wasn't 100% certain it was him, he also found out nothing in the handwriting of the letters to suggest that Arthur was not the author. He also confirmed that the fingerprints found on the letters, and on various objects at Rook Farm, had belonged to Arthur.

After a brief recess, it was time for Nizam to give his version of events. And while he seemed nervous and shy, his testimony gave the trial a completely different direction.

Nizam's testimony

What came out in Nizam's testimony was that he was in every way unlike his brother. Where Arthur was showy, confident and immensely proud of himself, Nizam was anything but. He was a very quiet man, whose voice during court proceedings was practically non existent. The judge suggested a small microphone, which Nizam then wore around his neck for the duration of the trial.

Nizam almost seemed lost and confused during his time giving testimony. He seemingly had no interest in providing an alibi for his brother, or even for himself. In fact, he didn't seem to like his brother at all. During his opening questions, Nizam's lawyer- Mr Draycott- established that the relationship between Nizam and his brother was based on fear. Nizam's first words to the court were: "I was afraid of him." He painted a picture of Arthur that his brother surely wouldn't like; one where he, Arthur, had wanted to kidnap and kill Muriel while Nizam was only a pawn in his game.

Nizam essentially confirmed everything that the prosecution suspected. He hardly tried to deny it, although he couldn't bring himself to admit it- but to the jury, who sat through him breaking down in tears and weeping time and time again, the two are hardly dissimilar. Towards the end of his time in the dock, the Attorney General asked Nizam why he didn't contact the police about the kidnapping he was blaming his brother for; like always, the answer came back, "I was scared..." His last words in his own defence were "I'd rather die than be charged with murder!", after which, he broke down weeping inconsolably.

The summary

The Attorney General summarised in a matter of fact, and relatively short, manner. He started by saying that while the case seemed relatively simple on the surface, it was anything but. His summary was very short, but he instructed the jury to do nothing but judge the case on the available facts and the interpretation of the law as provided by the judge. These facts included the fingerprints found on the ransom notes, as well as the logic of the case. "If you are satisfied there are such circumstances as render the committing of the crime certain, that there is no rational hypothesis except that the crime was committed, then you are entitled to conclude that she was murdered."

Mr Hudson, Arthur's defence attorney, told the jury that if there was any shred of doubt, then they ought to find both brothers not guilty. Clearly the fact that there was no body worked in his favor, as the fact that there was no body and no clear murder weapon meant that the case was a lot harder to solve. "All human beings are vulnerable. Don't allow your anger at an ordinary woman being brutally kidnapped, at the anguish of those near and dear to her ... don't let it affect your reason! Because it has taken place, we all want the people responsible to be brought to justice. But only if you are sure... It must be something of which you are sure."

Mr Draycott gave a similar summary, but crucially, told the jury to consider Nizam separately to his brother. "Don't approach it as 'the Hoseins', 'the brothers', unless the evidence compels you to it. ...The whole thing is the plan of a mind that has no understanding or grasp of reality." He was pointing the finger at Arthur; Arthur's larger than life personality, his grandiosity. All in comparison to Nizam's quiet demeanor. While he didn't come out and say it directly, he insinuated that Nizam had been practically compelled by his brother into murdering McKay.

The judge summed up his part in the case by telling the jury to be careful. Only once the brothers' role in the kidnap could be established, could they begin to consider whether they had murdered Muriel. After a brief statement, he sent the jury on their way; it took them from around noon until 4pm that day to reach a decision.

Both brothers were found guilty, unanimously, on every charge. But the foreman of the jury remained standing after having informed the judge of their decision; he recommended that Nizam be shown leniency. After the foreman spoke his part, Arthur was allowed to speak his, accusing the judge and jury of having committed a grave injustice against an innocent man. Becoming more and more incoherent and angry, he was eventually calmed down by the warders standing around him.

Having heard the jury's decision, the judge moved straight on to sentencing the pair. Arthur Hosein was sentenced to life imprisonment for murder, 25 years for kidnap, 14 years for blackmail, and a further 10 years just for sending the ransom letter. Nizam Hosein received a similar sentence, except minus ten years, as he was indeed given a more lenient sentence by the judge.

Because of the intricacies of the British justice system, their sentences were to run concurrently. And generally, given good behavior, sentences are normally reduced by a third. As such, it was expected that Nizam would be jailed for ten years, and Arthur for around seventeen.

What of the brothers today?

After twenty five years, Nizam was released from prison. He left Britain as soon as he was freed, and went back to live on the island of Trinidad. He lives at the family's home in a small town called California, on the western coast of the island. As of 2009, he was working for a business in a nearby city; reporters for a Trinidadian newspaper paid a visit to his home, but found that he probably wasn't there at the time.

His neighbors told the reporters that he hadn't been seen in a long time. "He comes and goes, and hangs out in east Trinidad," one of them said. Nobody answered the door when they tried knocking. Presumably, he wanted to lead a private life and to forget about his life in England, and in prison. If he is still alive today, he would be 69 years old.

Arthur died in prison. He had been consistently denied parole, and had complained to the European Court of Human Rights in both 1985 and 1996. He had been kept in a high security hospital near Liverpool since falling ill. He complained to the ECHR that he lost his right to have his sentence reviewed for over twenty years, as a result of having become mentally ill during his time in prison. The Home Secretary himself had had to deny Hosein the right to a review in September 1994.

He claimed, at that point, that he was no danger to either himself or others. He had long since passed his tariff, and presented no risk to the public, so he believed that he ought to be allowed at least to go through the Parole Board's review. The details of when and why he was sent to Ashworth Hospital are unclear, but in his complaint to the ECHR, neither he nor his lawyer objected to the fact that he was detained there on correct legal grounds.

His complaint was denied each time. He had suffered with mental and physical health problems, and died in 2009 at Ashworth Hospital.

THE MISSING SODDER CHILDREN

DOROTHY MILES

The 1945 Christmas Eve Tragedy of Fayetteville, West Virginia and The Missing Sodder Children

On Christmas Eve 1945, a fire consumed a two-story house timber house outside Fayetteville, West Virginia that was occupied by George Sodder, his wife Jennie, and nine of their ten children (the oldest, Joe, was serving in World War II at the time.) Yet, the story has never been solved and there are still questions that haunt both the town of Fayetteville and the remaining Sodder child, Sylvia Sodder Paxton, is still hunting for the truth and trying to answer the question that has haunted the family and many for 62 years.

What happened to the remaining children: Maurice (14), Martha (12), Louis (9), Jennie (8), and Betty (5)?

Were they kidnapped by people who were angry at George Sodder's criticism of Benito Mussolini? Were the victims of a kidnapping scheme that while illegal, was simply overlooked by the police, much like the case of Georgia Tann's selling of children?

Those who survived the Christmas Eve fire included: George (50), Jennie (?), John (23, who was fighting in World War II), Marion (17), George, Jr. (16), and Sylvia (2).

A History of George Sodder

George Sodder was born in Tula, Sardinia, Italy in the year of 1895. In 1908, he immigrated to the United States through Ellis Island with his older brother who returned to Italy after he cleared customs. Sodder (born Soddu,) spoke little of his life in Italy or why he had left his hometown. Nor was it ever explained why his older brother returned to Italy after clearing customs at Ellis Island. However, it was well-known that Sodder had strong feelings against Benito Mussolini and was outspoken regarding his criticism of the Italian Fascist Dictator.

Sodder first found work in Pennsylvania, where he brought water and supplies to those who the railroad workers. He later moved to Smithers, West Virginia for a more permanent position as a driver. This soon ended up with him owning his own trucking company. In the beginning, he hauled fill dirt to construction sites, but later began hauling coal that was being mined in the West Virginia coal mines. It was during this time that he met Jennie Cipriani, also an Italian-immigrant and the daughter of a storekeeper's daughter, who later became his wife.

George and Jennie settled outside of the town of Fayetteville, West Virginia, in Fayette County in a two-story timber-frame house approximately two miles north of the town. They chose this location partly due to the large population of Italian immigrants already living there.

Their first child, Joe, was born in 1923 and they would go on to have nine more children. During this time, George's business was doing well and they were a well-respected middle-class family in the area. One of his most passionate topics was that of Benito Mussolini, who became the youngest Prime Minister of Italy in 1922 and within five years he had, in effect, transformed Italy into a one-party dictatorship.

In a small town like Fayetteville, George Sodder's outspoken criticism of Mussolini did not go over well in the predominately Italian-American community where he and Jennie lived, and he had more than his share of arguments and had made some enemies due to his outspoken criticism of Mussolini. Many pre-World War II Italian Americans saw Mussolini as a strong leader who had succeeded in making Italy great again. However, George had strong opinions on a variety of subjects and was not shy about discussing them in public which often led to him alienating people, and threats were made against him and sometimes his family.

In 1943, Sylvia, the youngest, and last, of the ten Sodder children, was born and the eldest son, Joe, was fighting in World War II.

Christmas Eve, 1945, The Night of the Fire
Christmas Eve was celebrated much like most families of the era did. The eldest daughter, Marion, was working at a dime store in downtown Fayetteville and she brought home surprises for three of her younger sisters, Martha age 12, Jennie, age 8, and Betty, age 5. As it was Christmas Eve and the girls were so excited with the unexpected gifts, Jennie told them that they could stay up later than usual. Yet, Jennie told them at 10:00 pm that they could only stay up so long as the two oldest boys, 14-year-old Maurice and nine-year-old Louis, were still awake.

Although we don't know exactly what time Jennie went to bed for the night, she carried two-year-old Sylvia upstairs and went to bed herself. At 12:30 am the phone rang and Jennie woke up, went back downstairs, and answered it. She did not recognize the voice nor the name that the unknown female caller asked to speak with and told the woman that she had reached the wrong number. In fact, the only thing that Jennie recalled that was strange about the call was that the woman had a strange laugh.

As Jennie was going back upstairs to return to bed she noticed that the downstairs lights were still on and the curtains were not drawn which was something that they children normally did when they stayed up later than she had. Marion was asleep on the couch in the living room and Jennie assumed that the other children had gone up to the attic, where their bedrooms were.

At 1:00 Jennie was again awoken by a noise that sounded like something hitting the roof of the house with a bang, followed by a rolling noise. Assuming it was nothing important, she rolled over and went back to sleep. Yet, in half-an-hour she again awakened to the smell of smoke. The room that George used as an office was on fire, centered around the telephone line and the fuse box. Jennie woke up George, who then went and woke up his oldest sons. The parents, George and Jennie escaped from the burning house as did Marion, Sylvia, and the two older boys. Although the family yelled to the children still upstairs inside the house, they heard no response and were unable to reach them as the stairway was in flames.

Why was Rescuing the Other Children Impossible?

The phone at the Sodder house was engulfed in flames so Marion ran to a neighbor's house to alert them to call the fire department. By coincidence, a passerby did see the fire and tried to alert the fire department, but that was unsuccessful as well as either the phone at the tavern was broken or the operator was unreachable. Finally, the neighbor who Marion had awakened drove into town and called Fire Chief F.J. Morris who began to use what was then the "fire alarm" in Fayetteville. The "fire alarm" consisted of a "phone tree" where one firefighter would call another, who called another, who called another, and so on.

While the house was engulfed in flames George Sodder climbed the wall of the house and broke a window into the attic, cutting his arm in the process, intending to use the ladder that was usually resting against the house to rescue the children that were trapped in the attic. However, the ladder was not in its usual spot and they were unable to locate it anywhere nearby. The water barrel that could have been used to extinguish the flames was frozen solid and therefore was unable to be lifted, let alone able to put out the fire. Finally, in a desperate measure, George maneuvered his trucks so that they were next to the house, hoping to use them to climb up to the attic window, but neither of the trucks would start, although they had been working fine a day earlier. Within 45 minutes the entire home was destroyed and still smoldering.

Although the fire department was only two and one-half miles away from the Sodder home, the crew did not arrive until 8 am, at which time the house had been reduced to ashes. Fire Chief Morris said that the response was slower than normal because he, the Fire Chief, was unable to drive the fire truck and he had to wait until someone who could drive it was available. When the firefighters did arrive, there was little they could do but look through the ashes of what was once the Sodder's basement. By 10:00 Chief Morris told the family that there were no bones or fragments of bones that would have been expected to be found.

However, another source stated that bone fragments and internal organs were found but the Sodder Family was not told of this. Regardless, modern fire investigators feel that the search was incomplete as best, and with today's science it does not make sense.

George Sodder was told by the state's fire marshal to leave the site undisturbed so that a more in-depth investigation could be conducted. But within four days Sodder and his wife could not handle seeing the site anymore and George bulldozed five feet of dirt over the site as they intended to convert it to a memorial garden for the lost children. The picture on the right is the beginning of the memorial to the missing Sodder Children.

A memorial was constructed and in the 1950's a billboard was constructed with pictures of the missing children that remained until the death of Jennie Sodder in the late 1980s. The picture on the left shows George and Jennie standing in front of the billboard that stood for around 30 years (from the 50s until the late 1980s.)

The coroner convened a local inquest the day and it was found that the fire was caused by faulty wiring. There are many problems with this finding, the most troubling was that one of the jurors was a man who had "threatened George Sodder that his house would be burned down and his children 'destroyed" in retribution for his Anti-Mussolini remarks"

George and Jennie always believed that their children had been kidnapped, possibly by the Sicilian Mafia due to George's outspoken criticism of Mussolini and the Fascist government of Italy, and the "official findings" of the authorities did not change their minds.

Questions Before and After the Fire

Arson or Not? – while the Fire Department ruled that the fire was caused by arson, yet Sodder had recently had the house rewired and inspected;

In October 1945, a life-insurance salesman visited the Sodder home and after being turned down told Sodder that his house "[would go up in smoke...and your children are going to be destroyed." He blamed these remarks on the things that Sodder had been saying against Mussolini;

A separate visitor to the house, who it is assumed was looking for work, told Sodder that the fuse boxes in the back of the house would "cause a fire someday." This naturally cause George confusion as the house had been rewired when an electric stove was installed and he had gone a step further by called the local electric company to ensure its safety;

In the few weeks prior to the fire, a strange car was noticed parked along a main street in town. It appeared to many that the occupants of the car were watching the younger Sodder children as they returned home from school; and

When cremated, bodies are exposed to temperatures of between 870° - 980° Celsius (1,600° - 1,800° Fahrenheit) and even at that heat bones do not disintegrate all the way. The organs of the body burn at a much lower temperature than bone does, and the likelihood that any organs would remain intact at even the heat that wood burns, 300° Fahrenheit, is suspicious to say the least, that anyone would even suggest that there would be intact organs still present.

Odd Circumstances found After the Fire

The Sodder's believed that their children were kidnapped and the fire was set intentionally to cover the crime scene. Although no bodies or fragments of bodies were found, death certificates for the five children were issued on December 30 of that year. The local newspaper, *The Fayetteville Journal,* stated that the bodies of the missing children had been found, but stated later in the same story that only part of one body was recovered. A funeral was held for the children on January 2, 1946.

The Sodder's began to question the authorities regarding the official findings regarding the fire in many cases. Questions raised include:

The authorities claimed that the fire was started because of an electrical problem; however, the family had lights up for Christmas decorations which remained lit at least during the early stages of the fire. Had the cause been an electrical problem then surely the Christmas lights would have gone out. Additionally, when Jennie went upstairs after the late-night phone call the lights downstairs were on, which could not have been possible had the fire been due to an electrical problem;

A telephone repairman informed the Sodders that the fire was not the cause of the non-working telephone. Instead, it had been cut by an individual who had climbed 14-feet up the phone pole and then reached two-feet away from the pole to cut the line. A man was seen stealing a block and tackle from the property and was arrested. He admitted to the theft as well as being the person who cut the phone line, as he thought he was a power line, however, he denied having anything to do with the fire.

Of course, there are no surviving records which identify the thief or why he would have wanted to cut the power lines to the house.

In 1968, Jennie stated that had the power line been cut there would have been no survivors;

Jennie then began to question the presumption that the bodies had been burned entirely during the fire. Especially as many of the household appliances were, while burned and destroyed, were still recognizable among the ash. Around the same time Jennie read a story of another house fire where seven people had perished, however, skeletal remains were found of the deceased. This convinced Jennie to begin somewhat macabre experiments where she would burn small piles of animal bones to see if they would be destroyed – although none ever were. A cremator told her, as I stated earlier, that human bones remain even after bodies are burned at 2,000° Fahrenheit (1,090° Celsius) for two hours which was far longer than the approximately 45 minutes that the Sodder house was ablaze; and

Then came the stories and witness of those who had seen the Sodder Children alive looking out of a car while the fire was still burning and another woman stated that she had served the children breakfast the morning after the fire in a car at a rest stop between Fayetteville and Charleston. There was also a car with Florida license plates in the area as well.

At a hotel in Charleston, two men and two women registered with four of the five children and stayed in a large room with several beds. The woman reported that the men appeared to be of Italian descent and stated that the she had tried to speak with the children but the men refused to allow her to do so and appeared hostile.

By late 1946, the Sodders were convinced that their children were, in fact, still alive.

The Sodders Call in J. Edgar Hoover and the FBI for Assistance

In 1947, George and Jennie sent a letter to J. Edgar Hoover, head of the Federal Bureau of Investigation and received a reply from Hoover himself which read "Although I would like to be of service, the matter related appears to be of local character and does not come within the investigative jurisdiction of this bureau"

The irony of this statement, as we know today, is that while Hoover was instrumental in centralizing fingerprints and laboratories to help fight crime, he also used his powers in abusive ways and used the FBI to harass political dissenters and activists. President Harry S. Truman once said that Hoover used the FBI as his own "secret police force...the FBI is tending in that direction

However, Hoover's agents did say that they would help the local police force with the investigation if they could obtain permission from the local authorities, yet the Fayetteville police and the local fire department refused to cooperate.

The Sodder's Hire a Private Investigator

Certain that their children were alive and had been kidnapped, the Sodder's hired a Private Investigator, C.C. Tinsley from a town called Gauley Bridge that is close to Fayetteville. Tinsley was the one who discovered that the man who had threatened them with a fire the previous year regarding George's remarks about Mussolini had been on the coroner's jury which had determined the cause of the fire to be an accident, thereby ruling out arson.

However, the most shocking and disturbing finding of Tinsley's investigation, was that Fayetteville's Fire Chief, F.J. Morris, had supposedly found a human heart while looking through the ashes of the remains of the Sodder home. According to Morris he had packed the heart in a metal box and buried it. Then Morris confessed this to his local minister, who confirmed the story to George Sodder. At that point Sodder and Tinsley, the investigator, went straight to Morris and confronted him with the story who told them that it was true and took the two men to the buried heart.

Sodder and Tinsley took the box with the heart in it to the local funeral director who examined it and declared that not only had the heart never been exposed to fire, but it was in all actuality quite fresh beef liver rather than a heart. Later, rumors came to the attention of Sodder and Tinsley that had been spreading around town for quite some time in which Morris had admitted that the box with the heart in it had not come from the fire.

The question remains however, was Morris trying to leave "proof" that at least one of the children had perished in the fire or, more likely, was he trying to cover up his incompetence. Morris, the Fire Chief, could not drive the fire truck of the department that he oversaw, the two-hour investigation of a fire, no matter the circumstances, is inadequate at best and would probably be criminal in today's day and age.

The Second Excavation

As sightings of the Sodder children continued to come in from citizens, Sodder began to take a more active role. Instead of sitting and waiting for sightings, he began driving around the country after seeing a picture of someone that looked like one of his missing children. He once drove to New York City after seeing a picture of a ballet dancer who looked like his daughter Betty.

In 1949, George Sodder convinced Oscar Hunter, a well-known Washington D.C. pathologist, to help oversee a new search of the remains of the house. A very thorough search, unlike the one done that had been conducted in 1945 immediately following the fire, artifacts were found that belonged to the children, as well as some coins and bone fragments.

These bone fragments were sent to a specialist at the Smithsonian, Marshall T. Newman, who determined that they were in fact vertebrae from the lumbar region of the same individual. Because the transverse recesses of the vertebrae were fused, Newman estimated that the individual would have been between the ages of 16 to 23. This finding is because the vertebrae normally fuse at age 23. At the time of the fire, the oldest of the five children who did not escape was Maurice, age 14. Additionally, these bones did not show that they had been exposed to any flame that would lead one to believe that they had been through a fire. It is also strange that only vertebrae were the bones that were found as there should have been entire skeletons or, at the very least the bodies larger bones such as the humerus and the femur bones.

It was concluded that these bones had most likely come from the dirt that George Sodder had bulldozed over the site in the days following the fire after the official rudimentary two-hour fire investigation. It is believed that the bone fragments had most probably come from a nearby cemetery, *Mount Hope,* and had arrived at the site when Sodder had bulldozed it, but it could not be confirmed how they were taken from the cemetery to the site of the Sodder family home. The bones were returned to Sodder in September of 1949 and the whereabouts are currently unknown to the public.

In 1950, the West Virginia Legislature held two hearings regarding the case, but Governor Okey L. Patteson and the state police superintendent W.E. Burchett closed the case at the state level after declaring it "hopeless."

The Family Continues to Search by Themselves

The family still did not give up and continued to search for their missing children without the help of the authorities. Flyers were printed and distributed offering a $5,000 reward for any information that would solve the case. That amount was soon doubled to $10,000 (an unbelievable amount of money in the 1950s.) While some leads did come from the flyers and the promise of money, the Sodders went even further.

In 1952, a billboard was erected along what is now State Route 16 near Ansted which became somewhat of a tourist attraction, and was certainly a landmark in Fayetteville, West Virginia until the late 1980s when Jennie died.

George followed up on the leads from the night of the fire and the lead at the motel in Charleston where two men, two women, and four children who appeared to be of Italian descent (although investigators did not find her to be credible as she came forward with the information five years after the supposed occurrence.)

George personally followed leads from St. Louis, where he had heard that Martha was being held in a convent), to Texas where people had overheard a conversation about a fire in West Virginia years prior, and even went to Florida where a relative of Jennie's had children who resembled his and required proof before he was sufficiently convinced that they were not his children. In 1967, Sodder went to Houston, Texas to investigate another tip because he had received a letter from a woman who had met a man who revealed that he was in fact Louis Sodder. She went on to say that she believed that both Louis and Maurice were living in Texas somewhere. Upon arriving in Houston, however, Sodder and his son-in-law, Grover Paxton, were unable to speak with her and while the police did find the two men that she had been referring to they both denied being the missing sons. Paxton always said that doubts remained in Sodder's mind for the remainder of his life.

The Photograph

One of the major pieces of evidence that furthered the belief that at least Louis was still alive was a letter that Jennie received in the mail in 1968, over twenty years after the fire. It was accompanied by this photograph .) The letter was postmarked in Central City, Kentucky with no return address on it. Inside was a picture of a 30ish-year-old man who looked like Louis who, had he survived, would have been in his 30s. On the back of the picture was written:

"Louis Sodder

I love brother Frankie

llil boys

A90132 or 35"

The Sodder's again hired a private investigator who left West Virginia for Kentucky but was not heard from again.

The photograph was the last evidence ever received or followed up on by George or Jennie Sodder. George died in 1969 and Jennie died in 1989. The billboard remained standing until after Jennie's death as seen by the following photograph, in which you can't help but notice that this is a family that has been looking for their loved ones for 30 years with little to no help from the authorities, and what help they did receive was inadequate at best.

Jennie never forgot the tragedy that destroyed her family and consumed much of her husband's life and wore only black as they did in the Victorian era as a tradition or mourning for the rest of her life while staying in the family home and tending her garden at the site of her former house. After her death in 1989, the family finally took down the billboard which had been a fixture in town and even a for approximately 30 years.

The surviving children, including their children, have continued to work to keep the case in the public over the years. They, and the older residents of Fayetteville, continue to believe that the Sicilian Mafia had something to do with the kidnapping of the children and were trying to extort money from George Sodder. They speculate that the children may have been "rescued" by someone who was aware of the planned arson by promising that they would be safe.

The youngest child at the time of the fire, Sylvia Sodder Paxton, was the last remaining survivor of the children from the night of the fire and has tried to quietly assist in solving the case. Her own daughter made the same promise to her mother in 2006. Today, thanks to the Internet, there has been renewed interested in this and other cold cases and a book was written by George Bragg called *"West Virginia's Unsolved Murders"* in 2012. On the 60th anniversary of the fire, in 2005, Stacy Horn did a segment on *National Public Radio* and believes that it likely that the children died in the fire; however, she said that if evidence were to come to light that they did not die then she would not be shocked.

There are numerous articles, episodes, podcasts, and theories regarding the fate of the missing Sodder children but after 60 years it is hard to believe that we will ever find the truth.

THE SEX SLAVE MURDERS OF SACRAMENTO

170

ANA BENSON

Sacramento, California has seen a fair share of gruesome crimes during the 1970s and 1980s. That city was the hunting ground of the Original Night Stalker who is still unidentified until this day. Richard Chase was also active in the area and he was nicknamed the Vampire of Sacramento due to the uncommon ritual which included drinking the blood of his victims.

So when Gerald Gallego and his partner in crime Charlene Gallego embarked on their rampage of kidnapping and killing young teenagers, they were just a couple of many depraved criminals who were on the search for the next target around the capital of California. What made Gallego so terrifying was the fact that he had an accomplice who lured in the teenagers he had selected and the way he committed the killings by having a complete control over them.

The Gallego case once again sparked the debate about what makes a serial killer and are some people more prone to violence than the others due to their genetics?

Early life

Gerald Gallego was born in Sacramento, California on 17th July 1946. He would spend the majority of his youth in a tiny town just north of the city called Chico. His childhood wasn't easy since the environment he grew up in was quite stressful for a young boy. Gerald's mother was a sex worker while his father was constantly in and out of a jail. His mother was constantly dating abusive boyfriends who could be quite aggressive towards Gerald.

However, Gerald's father was probably the main bad influence in his life even though Gerald never actually met the man. He was a violent criminal who was incarcerated at the time of his birth. The final blow came when Gerald Gallego Sr. was arrested in Mississippi for a vehicle theft. His temper was evident to everyone because he told the authorities that he would murder the first police officer he sees after he gets out of the prison. Gallego Sr. escaped the prison in 1954 while taking a guard as his hostage. The two of them were on a run and spent a couple of days together, hiding from the police. Once Gallego Sr. was sure that the prison guard was of no use to him, he shot the man in the head, killing him on the spot.

Gallego Sr. was once again arrested and put to trial. He received a death penalty for murdering a prison guard. He was executed in 1955 in a gas chamber. Gerald Gallego was still a young boy while this was taking place. His mother made up a story about why his father is not with them but the crimes of Gallego Sr. would haunt Gerald Gallego later in his life. The children in his school and neighborhood knew the truth and weren't kind to him either, labeling Gerald as a child of a murderer.

Gerald Gallego got into crime when he was in his teens. He would often go out with his half-brother, committing petty thefts and using recreational drugs such as sniffing glue or lighter fluids. He sexually assaulted a girl who was only six years old when he was thirteen. Since he was a minor, the judge sent him to a boy's school for juvenile delinquents. Gerald and his brother escalated pretty quickly. The police tracked the brothers down after a robbery which resulted in a car chase and exchange of bullets in the middle of a street. The sentencing was light once again and he was placed in Preston School of Industry located in Ione, California. Gerald made a decision to move closer to Sacramento with his brother after his parole and they continued to steal and cheat in order to survive.

Gerald Gallego got married for the first time in 1963 when he was only sixteen. His wife was five years older than him. Just four months after the wedding, Gallego's daughter Krista was born. The marriage was a failure and the couple got divorced quickly. Gerald fought to gain the custody of his first child and the judge gave him the rights to take care of Krista. He made a decision to send the little girl to live with his mother since she didn't really fit into his lifestyle. However, he did visit the girl pretty often and it would later be discovered that he abused Krista as well. It started when she was only six years old and would continue until the late 1970s.

Two years after the divorce, Gallego had a new bride. She was also older than him and worked as a waitress at one of Gerald's favorite bars. This woman was oblivious to Gallego's violent past so when he started physically abusing her and attacking her with pretty much anything he could find inside their home, she filed for a divorce.

It took Gallego a bit over a year to find his third wife who worked for a laundry service. Once she saw his real nature, the woman got out of the marriage as soon as possible. In 1969 Gerald was married for the fourth time to a nineteen years old girl. She also couldn't put up with the daily abuse from Gallego and asked for a divorce. She didn't know that she was pregnant with his child at the time. Gallego's second daughter was born after the divorce and she still doesn't know who her father really is.

Gerald was not giving up in his quest to find true love so he got married for the fifth time in 1974. His latest bride also worked at a laundry service and she was significantly younger than him. She did put up with his abuse for years and filed for a divorce in 1977.

In the end, Gerald was arrested for more than twenty times and he also spent some time in jail. When he was in his twenties, Gerald Gallego cleaned up his act a bit and worked as a truck driver. He later moved on to bartending. It is evident that his relationships with women were quite difficult and by the time he met his future accomplice, Gerald had seven failed marriages behind him. He would marry two of his ex-wives twice.

Meeting Charlene

Charlene Adel Williams was born in Stockton, California on 19th October 1956. Her upbringing was completely different from Gallego's because she came from a stable home with loving parents who were always there for her. She was very clever which showed in her academic records. However, Charlene did start abusing drugs and alcohol in her early twenties which led to a downfall. She was also desperate to find real love which is evident by two divorces she went through before her friends set her up with "a lovely bartender" Gerald Gallego in the summer of 1977.

The date was a success and the two became inseparable soon after. While there is no evident cause which might have prompted this good girl to trust Gallego blindly until the very end, it was clear that Charlene had a rebellious streak herself. While she might have appeared innocent to the majority of people, Charlene did experiment with various sexual fetishes which were suggested by her former husbands. Some of her friends would later say that she did it in order to keep them by her side.

Whatever the reason, Charlene was enamored with Gerald and would listen to every suggestion he made. She was ready to break every rule for him and it was clear that Gerald had found the perfect accomplice for his deviant plans.

The murders

Just one year after the first meeting between Charlene and Gerald, the two of them committed their first crime. Gerald was having personal problems at that time and he simply couldn't make love to Charlene which led him to believe that he needed an extra stimulant which would solve the issue for him. He had fantasies about having the so-called sex slaves in his home and he presented the idea to Charlene who didn't object. After all, he would abuse her every time he couldn't get an erection, putting all the blame on her. Gerald explained to Charlene that he would need to actually hunt down a female and capture her before locking her up and using her for his own pleasure.

While Charlene was a bit confused by this, she was still on board even though she wasn't certain about her own role in the process. Everything will be revealed to her after the couple drove to a mall in Sacramento and parked their vehicle in an adjacent parking lot. Gerald instructed her to go out and find a teenage girl who would fit his sex slave fantasies. Charlene bumped into Rhonda Scheffler and Kippi Vaught who were sixteen and seventeen at the time. She told them that there was some weed back in her Dodge van and invited the girls to come along and get high together. They agreed and followed Charlene back to the vehicle where Gerald was waiting.

Once Charlene opened a door, Gerald pointed his gun at the girls, commanding them to come inside which they did. He quickly tied their hands and legs. Charlene drove the van to Baxter, California which is a remote place near Sierra Nevada mountain range. Gerald sexually assaulted both girls and then shot each of them in the head. The mere act of tying the girls and making the other watch the rape of her friend tells a lot about the sadistic personality Gerald had. It is also clear that the girls were hit with a heavy object before the fatal shots. They left them in a ditch without even trying to conceal the bodies. Their lifeless corpses would be found two days later.

Two weeks after the first murders, Gerald's daughter Krista visited the police station in Sacramento. It took her years of torture to finally put an end to the sexual abuse she endured from her father. Krista accused Gerald Gallego of sodomy, incest, and unlawful sexual intercourse. Gallego wasn't ready to face the authorities now when he just started turning his deviant fantasies into reality so he told Charlene that they would be moving away.

The cooling off period lasted for less than a year. Charlene and Gerald got married in the meantime and moved to Houston, Texas. They used aliases and would often travel to Reno, Nevada. That is where the second set of murders occurred in June of 1979. The newlyweds were driving around Washoe County Fair which is pretty close to Reno. The modus operandi was almost similar to the first two murders where Charlene was supposed to talk the girls into coming to her van. Since she was a young woman, the victims felt safe around her without sensing any impending danger.

Charlene started talking to Brenda Judd and Sandra Colley who were thirteen and fourteen at the time of their abduction. They agreed to go to Charlene's van where Gerald greeted them with a pointed gun and told the girls to get into the van. Charlene was once again the chauffeur while Gerald raped the girls in the back of the vehicle. The assaults lasted for about two hours and once Gerald was done, Charlene parked the car and watched him drag the girls out. Gerald then bludgeoned the girls with a hammer proving once again that he enjoyed the power he had over his victims.

Since they were left on a desolate road somewhere in Nevada, the law enforcement didn't find their bodies for decades. Brenda Judd and Sandra Colley were considered missing at the time and the police didn't start a murder investigation in this case right away.

The third set of murders also occurred one year later. The Gallegos followed the same pattern as in the first abduction by choosing the victims in a mall. They were once again back in Sacramento. Stacy Ann Redican and Karen Chipman-Twiggs were in a bookstore that day and after Gerald picked them out from the crowd, Charlene approached them. The girls followed her to the van and were made to come inside by Gerald. Charlene was in the driver's seat, occasionally glancing back to see what Gerald was doing to the girls. He ordered the girls to get undressed which they did. Gerald needed the control over the girls because he loved the feeling of being commanding and supreme. Both Stacy Ann and Karen were brutally raped and then murder by a blunt force trauma to their heads. The police would uncover their bodies three months later in July of 1980.

Their seventh victim was Linda Teresa Aguilar who was hitchhiking alone on 6th June 1980 in Oregon. Linda was four months pregnant at the time of the abduction. The couple picked her up promising that they would drive her to wherever she was going to and Gerald sexually assaulted her soon after. Linda's body was discovered more than two weeks after the murder. The investigators noticed that she had head injuries and they also found traces of bonds on her wrists and ankles. It was evident that she was beaten with a rock and then strangled. Her body was buried so the most shocking evidence was the fact that Linda had sand in her nose and lungs which indicated that she was still alive as Gerald placed her in the shallow grave near Gold Beach.

The next murder happened on Gerald's birthday in 1980. This was the first time Gerald selected a woman he knew so the pattern of the killings did change a bit. Virginia Mochel was a bartender in a place which was frequently visited by Gerald and Charlene in West Sacramento. Virginia was abducted from a parking lot after she completed her shift. The woman was dragged into Gallego's van where he proceeded to violently rape her. She was so tired of everything he had done to her over the course of several hours that she ended up begging Gerald to kill her and end her suffering. He strangled Virginia Mochel and dumped her corpse near a pond in Clarksburg, California. She would be discovered by a couple of fishermen three months after the murder. Even though her body was almost completely decomposed, the investigators found traces of the fishing line which was used to subdue her. The cord was still around her neck which confirmed the suspicion that she was strangled.

Craig Miller and Mary Elizabeth Sowers were the last victims of Gerald and Charlene. On 2nd November 1980, Miller and Sowers were leaving a party and were standing by a road when a car parked in front of them. This was the first time that Gerald Gallego actually exited the vehicle first and pointed his gun at this young couple. He ordered them to get inside but luckily, their friend Andy who was nearby managed to write down the license plates which would be the key evidence in stopping this murderous duo. As he approached the car to see what was going on, Charlene jumped out and told him to go away. She was once again driving the vehicle and as soon as they got to a remote and dark place, Gerald ordered Craig to get out of the car. He obliged and Gerald shot him in the back of his head, killing him instantly. He didn't even bother to cover up the body and the car drove off. Charlene was ordered to go back to their apartment with Mary Elizabeth and they took her inside where Gerald proceeded to rape the girl. The assault lasted for hours and once Gerald was done, all three of them got back into the vehicle. They once again arrived at another secluded area where Gerald shot Mary Elizabeth.

The investigation and the arrest

Andy who was a friend of Craig Miller and Mary Elizabeth Sowers waited for the morning in order to see if they came home safely. When he found out the couple was missing, Andy contacted the local law enforcement describing everything he saw that night – two people in a vehicle who drove Miller and Sowers away. He also gave the license plate number to the police who began their investigation right away.

The plate number led the investigators to the address of Charlene Gallego's parents who told them that their daughter was using their car. The police were confused by their findings because Charlene's parents were upstanding citizens so they thought they got the wrong information. But they proceeded to question Charlene who denied having any connection to the abduction of the young sweethearts. However, when they dug deeper into her life, they discovered that her husband did have a criminal past. The pieces started to connect and the investigators got a search warrant for their house and vehicle.

Charlene agreed to give the keys of the car to the investigator who was on the scene and she behaved politely. Gerald was nowhere to be seen at the time. The investigator entered the vehicle but couldn't find a thing that would indicate foul play. Charlene was pregnant at the time so she excused herself by saying she had morning sickness. The detectives agreed and asked her to come back to the station when she feels better in order to continue her interview.

Since there were no bodies, the police still approached this as a missing person case. However, Charlene didn't arrive at the station for an interview so Gene Burchett who was a homicide detective at the time went back to the house of Charlene's parents to see if she was around. He was talking to them when he got the call about a discovery of a corpse. Burchett drove straight to the scene of the crime where he found Craig Miller's lifeless body. He realized that this case is way bigger than they initially though, especially now when Charlene was not at home and Mary Beth was still missing.

The detectives found Gerald's address and tried to track them down there but no one was home. They would soon find out that Gerald and Charlene were on the run because they knew that the police was after them. The investigators entered the apartment and found numerous guns and firearm neatly displayed all over the tables. There was a lot of ammunition laying around as well but they couldn't connect it to the murder of Craig Miller.

However, a fellow bartender who worked with Gerald Gallego called the police and told them that Gerald did shoot his gun inside the bar one night. The officers arrived at the scene and collected the bullet which linked Gerald's gun to the bullets found at the scene of Craig Miller's murder. They were now certain that Gallego was the one who killed the young student. But they still needed to track him down.

It appeared that the murderous couple was on the run from the police but they were running low on money. Charlene contacted her parents from Salt Lake City asking them to send her some funds through a bank. They did so without contacting the law enforcement so the couple continued to travel from one city to another. They were first in Denver, Colorado but soon relocated to Omaha, Nebraska. The Gallegos were once again broke so Charlene called her parents. They realized the severity of the crimes their daughter was involved in so they told the FBI everything they knew. FBI waited for Gerald and Charlene at the Western Union bank in Omaha because they knew they would pick up the money there. And sure enough, the Gallegos entered the building as scheduled. They were arrested without any fight. Both of them were transferred to California where preparations for a trial were under way. Since Charlene was pregnant she gave birth to Gerald Gallego's first son while in prison. Charlene's parents got the custody of Gerald Armond Gallego Jr.

The trials

The law enforcement knew that the Gallegos were probably guilty for more than two murders so they focused on Charlene during the interrogations. The detectives were pretty sure that she was the weaker link and that making Gerald Gallego talk would be almost impossible. After hours and hours of questions, Charlene made a deal with the police, agreeing to tell them all and also to testify against Gerald in his trial for a lesser sentence. Two trials were scheduled – one in California and one in Nevada. Nebraska refused to file any charges against the couple so there wasn't a third trial.

Charlene pleaded guilty to the murders of Craig Miller and Mary Elizabeth Sowers so she received a minimal sentencing of sixteen years and eight months. It is the lowest punishment for a first-degree murder in California state and the prosecutor wasn't happy with the end result but he understood the importance of getting the whole story, as well as having a very important witness to tell every single detail once Gerald's trial comes around. Charlene made the similar deal with the judge in Nevada, once again getting the lowest punishment. Everything was ready for the main trial because it was Gerald Gallego's turn to appear in the courtroom.

Showing his true narcissistic traits, Gerald Gallego refused the court appointed defense. Instead, he acted as his own lawyer, making numerous mistakes during the process. He failed to cross-examine many important witnesses while focusing solely on Charlene whom he questioned for nearly a week. From the very start, Charlene claimed that she was afraid of Gerald who would often physically abuse her. She said that she was almost his hostage because he had a full control of her bank account and she simply couldn't get away from their toxic relationship. Gerald would often blame her for everything he was doing to the other girls.

Charlene told the jury: "I tried to get away. I tried, and people, especially women, will say, 'well, if you want to get away you can always get away.' It's not that easy; it's not that easy at all. I don't know why Gallego didn't kill me because he sure tried."

On the other hand, Gerald told the courtroom that Charlene was more than willing to help him out with the killings. As a matter of fact, she was an active participant in the assaults as well. Gerald also accused Charlene of putting the entire blame on him in order to save herself. As the trial was nearing the end, Gerald took the stand which allowed the prosecution to ask him questions, debunking many of his claims.

On 21st of June 1983, Gerald Gallego received a death penalty in California for the murders of Craig Miller and Mary Elizabeth Sowers.

Now it was time to transfer him to Nevada and arrange a new trial for him over there. Gallego was accused of murdering Stacy Redican, Karen Twiggs, Brenda Judd and Sandra Colley in the state of Nevada. Despite the efforts of the local police enforcement, the bodies of Brenda Judd and Sandra Colley weren't found at the time. Charlene did provide the investigators with everything she knew about the location where they left the girls but she wasn't one hundred percent sure because the place itself was pretty desolate.

However, Charlene told the investigators to compare the rope from Gerald's car to the one which was used to bound Stacy Redican and Karen Twiggs. It was a perfect match and when combined with Charlene's testimony, the prosecution had a solid case against Gerald Gallego. He did make an important change for this trial and allowed Gary Marr to be his defense lawyer. They continued the same narrative as in California claiming that Charlene was trying to save herself by providing the courtroom with false testimony.

The jury found him guilty in just a little bit over two hours of deliberation. Gerald Gallego received yet another death penalty but this time it was in Nevada.

The aftermath

Gerald Gallego continued to say that he was innocent throughout the years of his incarceration. He did file a couple of appeals in which he protested his representation in court. Nevada Supreme Court allowed him a new hearing in 1999 and he once again received a death penalty. Gallego was held in Ely State Prison, Nevada up until his death on 18th July 2002. He died of rectal cancer which was untreated and managed to spread to his lungs and liver. He was moved to prison's medical center. Gallego was in terrible pain a couple of weeks before his death and spent his last moments under heavy medication.

Charlene Gallego became Charlene Williams in 1985 when she divorced from Gerald. She served her sentence and was released from Nevada prison in the summer of 1997. She moved away from the West Coast, leaving her parents in California. Even though she didn't say where she was going, Charlene promised to register herself as a felon wherever she settled down. It would be discovered in 2013 that she changed her name and was back in California with her new husband.